Dead Men's Bones

Other titles in the Hodder African Readers series

The Fearless Four	978 0340 940426
The Fearless Four: Hijack!	978 0340 940419
The Fearless Four and the Graveyard Ghost	978 0340 940358
The Fearless Four and the Smugglers	978 0340 940334
Dead Men's Bones	978 0340 940365
Twin Trouble	978 0340 940310
Sauna and the Drug Pedlars	978 0340 940402
The Power of Corruption	978 0340 940341
Magic, Mystery and Mister Prince	978 0340 940389
Time Bomb	978 0340 940327
God's Case: No Appeal	978 0340 940372
One Man, Two Votes	978 0340 940396

Dead Men's Bones

Dan Fulani

HODDER EDUCATION
PART OF HACHETTE LIVRE UK

Hachette Livre UK's policy is to use papers that are natural, renewable and recyclable products and made from wood grown in sustainable forests. The logging and manufacturing processes are expected to conform to the environmental regulations of the country of origin.

Orders: please contact Bookpoint Ltd, 130 Milton Park, Abingdon, Oxon OX14 4SB. Telephone: (44) 01235 827720. Fax: (44) 01235 400454. Lines are open 9.00–5.00, Monday to Saturday, with a 24-hour message answering service. Visit our website at www.hoddereducation.co.uk

First published in this edition in 2006 by
Hodder Education,
Part of Hachette Livre UK
338 Euston Road
London NW1 3BH

Impression number 5 4 3 2
Year 2010 2009 2008

Cover illustration by Roger Payne
Illustrations by Marjorie van Heerden
Typeset in 13/16 Bembo by Charon Tec Ltd (A Macmillan Company), Chennai, India
Printed in Great Britain by CPI Cox & Wyman, Reading, RG1 8EX

A catalogue record for this title is available from the British Library

ISBN-13: 978 0 340 94036 5

Contents

1
A Contract

Ben Seloma turned to his companion and looked him straight in the eyes. 'I'll do it,' he said.

'Good,' the other man replied, 'I knew you would. You will be doing yourself and your country a great service. Sign the contract and then we can celebrate.'

The man reached into the inside of his dirty jacket and pulled out some papers. As he put them on the table, they soaked up some of the Coca-Cola which had spilled when he had poured it out for Ben.

'Is that the cleanest contract you have?' Ben asked, staring at the dirty, wet pieces of paper. 'I want to go through those terms with you before I sign.'

'Of course, of course,' the man replied. 'Now let me see.' He put his hand inside his jacket pocket and pulled out a pair of spectacles.

'You are under contract for six months,' he said. 'During that time you will make about fifty dives at the place which we own, some ten kilometres down the coast from Conception Bay. You will do your best to bring up samples of geological specimens to the surface to help us in our search for oil. We will pay you one hundred and fifty thousand dollars at the end of that period.'

He paused, stared hard at Ben over his spectacles, and said very slowly, 'One hundred and fifty thousand dollars – a great deal of money.'

He turned his attention back to the contract. 'Should you have an accident we will, of course, pay the necessary medical fees etcetera. The rest; accommodation, food and the terms of service you already know. Now then, where's my pen?' He put his hand in his pocket a third time and took out a broken pen.

'Now, my friend, just sign here.' He pointed to a dotted line on the last page and handed the pen to Ben. Ben slowly started to write his name. As he did so, the damp paper parted and the pen went through it.

'Is this the best you can do, Mr Moagi? The contract you have given me to sign is torn and dirty. The pen that you have given me to sign it with is broken. If your office equipment is in such poor condition, it doesn't give me much confidence in your diving equipment. Is everything second-hand and second-rate? If so, you can count me out.'

Mr Moagi started at him, his eyes getting larger and larger in his fat, perspiring face. He gave his shoulders a shrug which lifted his big neck further out of his frayed and dirty shirt collar.

'Look, Ben,' he said, with a deep sigh, 'you are one of very few fully-trained deep-sea divers in this part of the world. You are, I know, out of work and need a job very badly. I own oil prospecting rights over a big area of the Namibian coast which could be very profitable. I will pay you well. You know I have the money.'

His eyes stuck out like a frog's as he repeated, 'I have the money.'

His appearance suddenly changed again, as his fat lips tightened and his eyes narrowed. He looks just like a snake about to strike, Ben thought to himself. I'd better be very, very careful when I deal with this man. He isn't to be trusted at all.

'What does it matter to you if the paper is torn or if my pen is broken?' Mr Moagi said. 'Does it really make any difference at all if the pen you sign the contract with is broken? I am giving you a chance to make a great deal of money. It would not be difficult for me to hand you over to the police and you know only too well that they would be very glad to see you.'

Ben knew that this was true. Mr Moagi held him in his power. If he wanted to, he could hand him over to the police and there was nothing that Ben could do about it.

'All right,' said Ben, 'I've told you many times why things turned out as they did.'

Mr Moagi stared at him so intently that Ben turned his head away. 'Don't be a fool. Even though *I* may believe you, the police won't. You want a job and you can't go to any other company, because you are wanted by the police. Whether you committed a crime or not makes no difference whatsoever. The fact is you cannot work for anyone else but me and you know it.'

Ben picked up the contract and turned over the last page. On a small, dry space, he wrote in large, carefully formed letters: 'I, Ben Seloma, accept your contract of employment.' He then dated it and handed it back to Mr Moagi.

There you are, Mr Moagi, the contract is signed. I am now in your hands; but I warn you, if you try to cheat me, I will never forgive you.'

The fat man burst into laughter. 'Oh well said, well said,' he shouted. 'Now, let us celebrate, for we have a great deal to celebrate about.' He turned round in his chair and called out, 'Anna! Anna! Come here at once.'

Moments later, a slim, attractive girl, in her early twenties, came through the office door. Without looking at Ben, she went up to Mr Moagi and, slightly bending one knee as a mark of respect, said, 'Yes?'

'Anna, my dear, bring us some beer. Ben and I have to celebrate. Ben is going to work for us with my oil research project.'

Anna said nothing and disappeared behind the door. In a few moments she returned, carrying a tray with beer bottles.

'Well done, my dear,' said Mr Moagi, as she put the tray down on the table. 'Now, Ben, have a beer.'

'No thank you,' said Ben, glancing down at his empty Coca-Cola glass. A fly had been struggling in the liquid which had been left in the bottom of the glass. Now it was dead. A shiver went down his spine. Maybe I'm about to die just like that fly, he thought to himself. In a trap of my own making.

2
A Mad Scheme

As Ben walked into the Walvis Bay offices of OFN, which stood for Oil for Namibia, he shivered in the coolness of the air-conditioning system. Just beside the entrance door was a large wooden table with a typewriter, a switchboard and a number of copies of popular magazines and daily newspapers. Behind this desk sat Anna.

'Hello there,' he began, 'I didn't know ...'

Anna interrupted Ben before he could finish his sentence. 'He's in the office over there and expecting you,' she said, pointing to a door to their right. 'Wait here.'

Without glancing at him, she picked up the receiver from the switchboard.

'Mr Seloma is here,' she said. Then, replacing the receiver, she nodded her head in the direction of the office door. 'He's waiting for you,' she said without a smile.

Ben grinned at her but without a further word she picked up one of the magazines, pushed her chair back, put her feet on the table and took no further notice of him.

'Come in,' said Mr Moagi, in answer to the knock on the door. He was sitting in shirt sleeves in front of a table fan. This was causing all the papers on his desk to be blown around. In spite of the air-conditioning, another much older fan groaned as it slowly turned overhead. The fitting was very loose. Ben could see the ceiling-board moving up and down as the fan turned.

Mr Moagi got to his feet and held out a fat, sweaty hand. 'Welcome. Welcome to your first day in my employment.' He walked over to a map fixed to the office wall. 'Come over here, Ben. I want you to look at this map. It is very accurate because it was prepared from a photograph which was taken by a satellite.'

Ben stared at the map which had been marked with coloured pencils.

'You see this area which is marked in red. That is the area which I have got for exploration. I want you to start your first dives in this section here.' Mr Moagi pointed to a blue circle within the red outline.

As Ben studied the map more closely, he saw that the whole area which Mr Moagi had got, and which he had agreed the previous day to explore, was covered with underwater rocks.

'How did you get this area?' Ben asked, turning to stare at Mr Moagi. 'Who gave you permission to look for oil? As far as I know no one else thinks there are deposits of oil along this coastline. No one has ever suggested that oil can be found here. Furthermore, you know how difficult it would be to extract oil if it was under those rocks. How can I collect geological samples from underneath rocks? No other major oil company in the world has any interest in looking for oil here. What makes you, of all people, think that you can become an oil millionaire?'

Mr Moagi wiped his hand across his forehead which, in spite of the fans and the air-conditioning, was sweating a lot. He looked at Ben and smiled.

'I've always been a gambler, Ben. I just feel that oil lies off those shores.'

'It's dangerous diving over rocks. I could get trapped down there. You're crazy; all you'll find is a heap of stones.'

'My boy,' said Mr Moagi, the smile disappearing from his face, 'remember the police and your

Mr Moagi showed Ben the diving area.

contract. We have a little agreement; all you have to do is to fulfil it for me.'

'I don't like the way you said that,' said Ben. 'It sounds very like a threat to me. I'm not going to stand here arguing with you. The scheme is crazy. My life is more valuable than your money. Say what you like to the police. I'm off!'

As he turned towards the door, he heard Mr Moagi pick up the telephone. Opening the door, he saw Anna hurriedly dialling a number on the switchboard.

He spun round and faced Mr Moagi. 'What are you doing?' he shouted. 'Taking me by force? You can't do that.'

'No, Ben, I'm not taking you anywhere,' Mr Moagi said, a cruel expression spreading across his fat face. 'It's the police who will be taking you somewhere, not me. As soon as they get Anna's message, they'll come along to talk to you. I am sure that they'll be very interested to see you. For my part, I'll not be sorry to see the back of you.'

Ben hesitated. There is very little that I can do, he thought. The police will never believe my story.

'All right, Mr Moagi,' he said, through clenched teeth, 'you win. Tell her to put back the receiver.'

Mr Moagi shouted to Anna, who replaced the telephone receiver.

Ben sat down on a chair and muttered, 'I'm ready, Mr Moagi. Tell me what you want me to do.'

'I'm so glad that you have come to your senses, Ben.' He fingered the sticky, dirty collar of his shirt. 'There's little more to say. You know the area where I want you to start diving. I believe that there's a good chance of finding oil, otherwise I would not be sending you down there. I want you to start as soon as possible. As you can see from the map, it's not very deep and the rock forms a reef which goes on for some distance above the seabed. You will dive with the kind of equipment you have used before and with which you will be familiar. A motor boat will take you out to the site.'

'I have worked for a crook before,' Ben said, 'but never for a madman. You know how quickly storms blow up at this time of year. Why didn't you start this job five months ago?'

The other telephone on Mr Moagi's desk suddenly started to ring and before Mr Moagi could answer the question, he had picked up the receiver. Ben could hear the voice at the other end shouting down the line.

'Mr Moagi, Mr Moagi, is that you? I want to talk to you, the others are ...'

Mr Moagi shouted into the receiver, 'Oh, it's you. I'll ring you later, Arnie.' He replaced the receiver and looked up at Ben, a thoughtful expression on his face.

'Ah, yes, Ben, what were you saying about the weather? I couldn't arrange things earlier. I had certain problems which had to be dealt with first. Don't worry, I've a feeling that everything will be all right and that we shall be very successful.'

'You place a great deal of confidence in your feelings. I certainly wouldn't trust them.'

Mr Moagi ignored this last remark. Ben noticed how distracted he had become since the last telephone call.

'Come back here at three o'clock,' Mr Moagi said, looking down at his large, gold wrist-watch. 'We shall go straight down to the jetty and take out the boat. You've got three hours to yourself. Now leave me please. I have work to do before we start.'

Ben turned and went out of the door. As he passed Anna, she looked away. As he let himself out of the main door, he distinctly heard Mr Moagi's voice saying to Anna, 'Get me Arnie in Jo'burg – and be quick.'

3
A Boat Trip

When Ben returned to the OFN office at three o'clock, neither Mr Moagi nor Anna was there. The office was locked and, having knocked loudly on the door a couple of times, Ben was turning to go away when he heard footsteps behind him. He turned round and faced a total stranger. The man was tall, very thin and wore a torn shirt and faded khaki trousers. Ben took an instant dislike to him and was about to walk away when the stranger spoke.

'Are you called Ben?' he asked.

'Yes,' Ben replied, looking at the man suspiciously.

'Good,' the other went on. 'We are setting out to sea right away.'

'Who are you?' asked Ben. 'Who sent you to fetch me?'

'Mr Moagi told me to find you and to take you with me.'

Reluctantly, Ben followed as the man led him down towards the waterfront. When they reached it, they did not stop but walked on along a road which led towards the outskirts of town. They came to a place where the tarmac ended and became a sandy track. After they had walked a further three kilometres, the man stopped by a rowing boat which was lying on the sand. He pushed the boat into the water and, as he did so, signalled to Ben to get in.

'Where do you think we're going in this?' asked Ben. 'This boat isn't fit to take us out to sea.'

'Get in,' commanded the man, without looking at Ben. 'The boss said that you have agreed to do what I tell you to do.'

Ben had by this time decided that it was useless to argue and so he climbed into the boat. The other man pushed it into the water and jumped in behind him. Having told Ben to sit in the back of the boat, he began to row them out to sea. The man started to sing: a sad song in a strange language which Ben did not understand. Over and over again he repeated the same song in time to his oars hitting the water.

They reached a shallow bay. Keeping close to the shore, they rowed round it. As they came back to the open sea, Ben could see a number of these small bays stretching into the distance. They went round one, then another and then another. The journey seemed endless and Ben had no idea where they were going.

'How much further?'

The man continued to sing.

'I said, how much further?'

'It's not far,' said the man, going on with his song.

They had been traveling in this way for a long time, when it suddenly occurred to Ben that it was madness to try to dive at this time of day. It would be dark by the time they reached the diving area. The sun was already sinking low in the sky.

Ben shivered in the chill of the early evening. The splash of the oars and the sound of the water flowing under the boat made him feel sleepy. He hugged himself tightly, swaying to and fro in time to the boatman's song. Still the man rowed on.

Ben thought back to the events which had brought him into contact with Mr Moagi. He thought about how Mr Moagi had been just a small trader in the town where Ben had been brought up. In fact, Mr Moagi's 'Shining Star Supermarket' had been the only place where you could buy matches, soap, kerosene and all the other things which people needed.

Everybody in the town knew Mr Moagi and most of them distrusted him. People said that Mr Moagi would sell his own mother if the price were right. Ben pictured the rusty, tin-roofed store which Mr Moagi had proudly called a 'supermarket'. He opened the store every day of the week, in spite of attempts by the mission to make him close on Sunday. Thieves and rogues spent the daylight hours gambling on the mud verandah whose rusting roof shielded them from the hot rays of the sun. At night, they no doubt took up their own bad business. It was often said that Mr Moagi received stolen goods from these petty crooks. It was said, but never proved, because the local inspector of police was his good friend and was often seen carrying boxes of beer out of the supermarket's back door.

Ben thought about his own education and how, in spite of a late start, he had soon become the school's most successful student, not at lessons but at sport. He had won cups for running and his biggest success was in swimming. No one in the town had ever known such a strong swimmer. 'He'll make the Olympics,' the school's headmaster had told his father.

Well, he thought, I never did and never will. Later events have seen to that.

Swimming was the reason why he was sitting here now. If it had not been for his success at swimming, he would never have won the scholarship with an oil firm to train in South Africa as a diver. If it hadn't been for swimming, he would not now be wanted by the police for . . .

A shout from the other man stopped these thoughts. He opened his eyes and in the distance he saw what looked like a camp fire on the far side of a tiny bay.

In the darkness the light from the fire acted as a beacon for them to steer by. As they drew closer to the light, Ben could hear people talking and could see them walking in front of the fire. The stranger called out in his own language across the water and there was an answering shout. They glided slowly up towards the shore and the bottom of the boat grated gently, as it hit the soft sand underneath.

'Welcome,' a voice called out of the darkness, and the boatman returned the greeting in a low voice. Two men on shore pulled the boat up and on to a sandbank. Ben and his companion jumped ashore. Behind the fire were four huts roughly built of branches and canvas. They looked as though they had only recently been completed. One was quite large, obviously some sort of communal hut; the others were probably used for sleeping.

The boatman took Ben by the arm and led him towards the largest hut. As they stood outside, Ben could hear Mr Moagi talking excitedly to another man inside the hut. By the side of the entrance was a notice which said: 'Oil for Namibia'. There was something rather odd about it and, as he passed it, he touched it. The paint was wet.

'Welcome, welcome,' said Mr Moagi, rising from a wooden packing case. 'Welcome to our offices. Welcome to headquarters.'

'You might have told me what your plan was before I was picked up by one of your men.'

'My dear Ben,' said Mr Moagi, sitting down on the case with a tired sigh, 'you're such a reluctant employee that if I had explained things in more detail you might never have taken up your duties at all. You were very reluctant to do so yesterday.'

'What on earth is the point of bringing me all the way out here at this time of night when we can't start diving until the morning? Why did you lead me to believe we were starting this afternoon? And why is that notice outside dripping with wet paint? Has this all been done for me? If so, forget it. We won't find enough oil here to fill an oilcan. Just what is going on here?'

'Questions, questions, always questions,' sighed Mr Moagi. 'We will find oil. It will fill more than an oilcan. But there is just one point I must make clear. We shall only be diving at night.'

'Diving at night!' Ben cried out in amazement. 'You're mad!'

The hut was lit by a single lamp and a moth was fluttering against the lamp's glass. Its efforts cast a shadow on Mr Moagi's face and gave him a very evil appearance.

Before either he or Ben could continue, a man, who had been crouching in the corner, stood up and said in perfect English, 'You will dive at night. That's all there is to it. You have done it before and you know quite well that it is possible to dive at night. Please follow me and stop your silly questions.'

Ben opened his mouth to argue, but as the man got up from out of the shadows he stopped himself. The man's face was completely covered in a black hood which had had slits made for the eyes and mouth. Before Ben could say anything, the man spoke again.

'Don't be scared of my appearance, Ben. I suffered a bad accident to my face some time ago and it is so much kinder to everyone if I keep it covered in this way. Come, follow me.'

As Ben left the hut, he noticed the moth drop to the ground, having finally burnt itself to death.

Without looking at Mr Moagi, he followed the hooded man out of the hut. He was taken round to one of the smaller huts. Outside the door, the man stopped and told him to go inside.

'You will rest inside and Anna will give you anything you want. We have much to do tonight. We shall be back for you in exactly one hour.' He slipped away as Ben bent down and entered the hut.

4
The Hooded Man

Anna sat in a corner slowly stirring a pot on a fire made out of a few twigs. Ben blinked in the smoke-filled atmosphere. When his eyes had grown used to the smoke, he noticed that Anna was dressed in a simple cloth. Gone was the smart suit. She wore no shoes and her hair was plaited in the local fashion.

'Hello again,' said Ben. 'Although you don't want to talk to me, you might try and say "hello". After all, you and Mr Moagi are stuck with me for six months and there's nothing that either of us can do about that.'

Anna said nothing but continued to sit by the pot. Slowly she stirred the contents.

'Maybe you can tell me what's going on here. Nobody else will. What are these madmen doing, sending divers to look for so-called oil in the middle of the night? Everybody knows that there is no oil in this area.'

Anna looked up at him. 'If you want something to eat, it's here,' she said, without showing any sign of emotion. She then got up, pulled the cloth tightly around her body, and left the hut.

Ben sat down. It seemed that he was more of a prisoner than an employee. How would he get through the next six months? He would be lucky if Mr Moagi paid him and, if he didn't, there was nothing Ben could do. Mr Moagi knew all about his problem with the police.

A fly buzzed around his head and he swatted it away. He cursed himself for having been such a fool to get mixed up with Mr Moagi. Knowing about Mr Moagi's own past, it might have been better if he had gone to the police himself and given himself up.

About twenty minutes later, Mr Moagi returned. He waddled into the hut and stood staring at Ben, with his hands on his hips. 'Well, Ben,' he said, 'get ready; it's time to go.'

Ben got up and followed Mr Moagi outside. As they walked down to the sea-shore, the air seemed very still and there were flashes of lightning in the sky. A storm will be coming soon, not today, maybe not tomorrow, but soon, Ben thought.

How can they be so stupid as to start diving at this time of year?

A motor boat was moored close to the shore. It was very light and could travel very fast. It was right for crossing the little bays but not for heading out to the open sea.

'Are we going out there in that?' Ben asked. 'Are we a suicide squad?'

Mr Moagi said nothing but signalled him to go on board. As Ben did so, he noticed the boatman. It appeared that he was going to take them out to sea.

'Are you coming with us, Mr Moagi?' Ben asked. 'If you do, we might all sink.'

'No, my friend will join you in a minute,' answered Mr Moagi.

'What, the hooded one?' asked Ben, with some alarm. 'We're not going to sea with him, are we?'

'Yes, and he's no fool, in spite of his unusual appearance,' said Mr Moagi. 'Don't worry, he knows exactly what he's doing, where he's going and what we're looking for.'

'What are we looking for?' asked Ben. 'Whatever it is, it's certainly not oil. You must think that I'm very stupid if you think that I believe that.'

'Of course we're looking for oil,' said Mr Moagi angrily. 'How many times do you have to be told? Ah, here he comes now. If you go into the cabin you'll find all the diving equipment you'll need. I'd also be careful what you say, if I were you,' shouted Mr Moagi. 'My friend has neither the sense of humour nor the patience that I have.'

Ben opened the cabin door and went inside. The light was on. At least the boat's batteries had been charged, he thought. On the floor, neatly laid out, was a full set of diving equipment, six large oxygen cylinders and an underwater light to strap around his head. He checked the pressure in the cylinders and found that they were full. The suit and other equipment seemed new. At least that's something, Ben thought.

Mr Moagi and the man in the hood were talking in low whispers on the shore. They were speaking too softly for him to hear, although he did hear Mr Moagi say that time was short. A few minutes later the hooded man climbed on to the boat deck and, having given a brief order to the boatman, entered the cabin. He didn't look quite so frightening to Ben in the bright inside light.

Ben turned towards him as he entered. 'Right, it's all yours,' he said. 'Get us there and get us back. I'll do the diving, you do the steering.'

'Now, Ben,' the man said slowly, 'just remember one thing. I give the orders round here, not you.'

He went over to the controls and pressed a switch. The engine sprang into life.

Ben looked back towards the little camp as they accelerated towards the open sea. He watched as the light from the fire grew smaller and smaller and then disappeared. It was very calm and still. He went on the deck and watched the lightning flashing in the distance.

Once or twice he thought he heard the faint rumble of thunder and as he did so he shivered. The boat carried a strong searchlight which shone out clearly about twenty metres ahead of them. They had been travelling for almost half an hour when suddenly the throttle was turned right down and, as the engine died, Ben saw a marker buoy bobbing in the water. This was obviously the spot that they were heading for. They drifted close to the buoy and the boatman threw a rope over its top and tied the boat to it. At this point the hooded man came out of the cabin.

'Get into the suit, Ben, and don't take too long about it.'

Ben nodded and went back inside the cabin. He noticed that a map had been spread out on the table. He glanced at it and saw an underwater reef which had been circled with a heavy line in red. In the centre a large cross had been made and Ben guessed that this must be the spot where they were now. None of it makes sense, he thought, as he took off his clothes and put on the diving suit. He put on the rest of the equipment and then checked the oxygen cylinders.

'I'll want some help putting these on,' he called out. The hooded man spoke to the other man who entered the cabin and strapped the cylinders on to Ben's back. Ben then picked up the headlamp, tested it, and pointed to the lamp and to his head. The hooded man strapped it on.

'Well,' he said, as he turned to face his two companions, 'will you please tell me, in plain and simple English, just what this is all about and what I am supposed to be doing when I dive under the water?'

5
The Shipwreck

'We've told you many times that we are looking for oil-bearing geological specimens,' said the hooded man. 'I want you to go down there and tell us exactly what you find. No more and no less, just exactly what you find. And please, for the sake of our friendship, please be absolutely truthful. It will save trouble in the long run.'

'I wish you would stop talking in riddles,' muttered Ben. 'Then we would all get along a good deal faster. All right, I'll do that. I'll go for a swim and I'll tell you everything that I see. Rocks and fishes, no doubt. I can tell the difference, you know.'

'Good. I'm glad that you are being helpful at last,' the hooded one went on. It seemed to Ben that his voice came from the pit of his stomach. He shuddered to think what lay behind the man's mask.

'We have a winch at the back of the boat with a cable to lower you down and bring you up again. The signal for your return will be for you to pull twice quickly on the cable. We will then wind you up. Now get going, time is moving on.'

Ben went to the stern of the boat where the boatman was turning the handle of the winch which released the cable.

'Tell your friend to do it steadily and slowly,' Ben said, 'and don't try winching me up before I'm ready.' He put the diving mask on his face and switched on his headlamp. Then he grasped the cable and was carefully lowered over the side of the boat.

As he disappeared under water, the light from his headlamp lit up the water in front of him. For a moment he could see only the bubbles he had created as he had gone in, but as the cable was released and he sank deeper and deeper, the bubbles disappeared and he was surrounded by blackness.

He had done this many times before, in far more dangerous situations, but he felt more uneasy about this dive than any other dive that he had made in the past.

After what seemed like a long time, his feet touched something solid. Looking down, he could see that he was standing on the top of a large, rocky outcrop. This is the reef, he thought to himself. Although he couldn't see very far ahead of him, he realised the possible danger. So sharp were the rocks, that he knew he could easily cut his suit or trap an ankle in one of the many holes and crevices.

Ben looked at the large luminous and waterproof watch which he always wore when diving. He needed to keep a careful check on the time so that he did not run out of oxygen. He tied the end of the cable to a piece of rock and carefully started to walk along the top of the underwater reef.

This is madness, he thought to himself. Here am I, risking my neck for nothing, absolutely nothing. Nevertheless, he knew in his heart that there must be a very important reason why they wanted him to explore the reef. They certainly had no reason to kill him, so they must be after something. It certainly wasn't oil, so what was it?

The rocky outcrop along which he was walking suddenly dropped away into what appeared to be a deep, black hole. He decided to walk round the edge of the hole until he had returned to the place where he had tied the cable. The hole seemed to be very wide, as well as very deep, and it was not until he reached its very edge that his headlamp was able to shine down into it. Then, with alarming suddenness, he saw it. His powerful light picked it out section by section.

At the bottom of the hole lay the wreck of an old, three-masted sailing ship. The masts were broken, the decks were splintered and there was a large, jagged hole in its side. So that's what they're after, thought Ben.

He could tell by the pounding of his heart and the growing pressure on the sides of his head that his oxygen was running out. He had better get back fast. Glancing at his watch, he realised that he had only a few minutes left before the oxygen would be finished.

He retraced his steps and came to the place where he had tied the cable. He struggled to untie it and, when he had eventually done so, he gave it two hard tugs.

The cable was quickly pulled upwards with Ben hanging tightly to it. He broke the surface and strong hands helped him over the side of the motor boat. He pulled off his diving mask and lay gasping for air on the deck. He had only just made it. A few seconds later and his oxygen would have been finished.

'Well,' the hooded man said, 'you cut that a bit fine. You must have found something interesting.' He paused. 'Well, did you?'

For a moment Ben was tempted to say that he had seen nothing except some rather interesting rocks and fishes, but the urge to tell his story was too great.

'Yes, I saw it,' gasped Ben. 'I saw the wreck. It's there all right, but a long way down. It's stuck in the middle of a hole in the reef. Will you please tell me the name of the ship, how long ago it sank and what you're trying to get from it?'

'Well,' the hooded man said, 'that's good news, and on your first dive, too. Mr Moagi will be pleased. You see, we had to let you find out for yourself, otherwise we would never have known if you were tricking us. Having found the wreck, I can now tell you its history. It was a slave-trader, trying to sail to the Caribbean with its slaves nearly two hundred years ago. It was called the *Golden Queen* and was trying to sail from Mombasa, round the Cape to Trinidad. Not many ships took this route and very few of those that made the attempt survived. The *Golden Queen* struck the reef and sank.'

'But what use is it to you?' asked Ben.

'The old records show that the ship was carrying treasure. It's treasure we are after. It's the reason that you will return to the wreck.'

'You want me to go back down there?' Ben asked. 'Do you know what you are saying? That ship is stuck in a deep hole a long way below the level of the reef. If I get trapped down there I'll die. I don't intend to take the risk. Anyway, why isn't the Namibian government undertaking the investigation? Why are you keeping the whole affair so secret? I suppose it's because you want the treasure for yourselves. If the government found out about it, you would have to hand any treasure over to them.'

'Precisely,' replied the hooded man, with a degree of honesty which surprised Ben. 'That's why we won't stop because of a change of mind on your part. You will continue to dive for us, otherwise we will kill you. I am being quite serious. You already know too much. You could easily become a risk to us.'

'What do you think ...?' Ben began, but stopped when he saw the gun which the man had pulled out of his pocket. As he glanced over towards the other man, he saw that he, too, was armed.

'So, that's the way it is going to be, is it?' Ben said. 'It seems that I am out-numbered and out-gunned. You certainly mean business, don't you? Who would have thought that Mr Moagi, the dealer in soap and matches, would have dared to get into something as dangerous as this?'

In spite of this brave speech, Ben was frightened. He had led an adventurous life but he had never before had two loaded pistols pointed at him.

'Put your guns away,' he went on. 'I'm not going to argue with you, as I am in no position to do so. Put them away and let's talk about what you want me to do.'

The hooded man said something and the two men lowered their guns.

'That's better,' said Ben. 'That's more friendly. As far as I can see, there are two main points. One, if you want me to go back down there I will need an extra oxygen cylinder so that I can stay under the water longer. Two, this will mean I will be carrying more weight; making it difficult for me to move around. So I will have to be dropped right over the wreck itself. It's going to be very dangerous going straight down into the hole, so I'll have to be dropped in exactly the right place. We'd better take another look at the chart to see the exact dropping point.'

In spite of his dislike of the other two men, Ben was becoming caught up in the excitement of the job. He had never dived for treasure but he had known other divers who had done so. He had felt the thrill of adventure when they had told him their stories, and the descriptions of the coins and jewellery that they had found. The sailing-ship that he had seen was a large one. It would take time to explore it thoroughly. It was almost beyond the ability of one diver to do so and bringing up heavy metal objects from the seabed was not easy. Nevertheless, he was so excited he forgot that he was being forced to dive, whether he wanted to or not.

A flash of lightning lit up the scene for a brief moment and a gust of cool air swept across the sea. He shivered and said to the hooded man, 'These storms are going to break before too long. We had better get on with the job. What time is it?'

'Eleven o'clock,' the other replied. 'We'll be able to fix you up with the extra oxygen. Let's go and look at that chart.'

Inside the cabin, he noticed the gentle rocking movement of the boat as the wind started to disturb the sea. There was a gentle lap, lap, as the waves splashed against the motor boat's sides. Ben thought again just how weak the boat would be in a storm.

The two men bent over the map, which showed in great detail the rock formation which lay on the seabed. Outside, the other man had started to sing his song again.

'That's where I went down,' Ben said, pointing to the cross on the map which indicated the marker buoy. 'That's the part I walked along and that must be the hole where the ship is stuck. I'm sure I'm right. Have you a coloured pencil so that I can mark it?'

The other man handed him a blue pencil and Ben carefully circled the spot where he felt the ship must lie.

'Now, let's take a measurement. Yes, that's it, about fifteen metres on a line north, north-west from the buoy. That's the spot where you'll have to lower me down.'

The lapping sound was growing louder. The other man's song seemed to have quickened to keep up with the movement of the sea.

'Hey,' Ben cried out in alarm, 'the wind's getting stronger. We have no time to lose. If a storm breaks tonight, then we're in real trouble.'

Ben realised that he was taking command of the operation. The hooded man seemed to be falling in with his plans and instructions. In a few minutes they had replaced the empty cylinder with full ones. Ben hated going down with two cylinders, as it was like a dead weight on his back and made walking difficult. The other man untied the cable from the buoy. They switched on the engines and steered the boat to the point which Ben had made on the chart, and under which he felt certain that the wreck must lie.

'You've got to keep the boat over this point,' he said. 'It's going to be difficult in this rough sea but you must do it. As soon as I reach the wreck, I'll tie up the cable as best I can but, if the strength of the wind increases, it will put a great strain on the cable. Whatever you do, don't let the boat drift away from this point. Do you understand?'

'Yes.'

Out on deck Ben took hold of the cable. He could see that the waves were now bigger and that spray was being blown over the side of the boat. There was no time to lose. He switched on the headlamp, swung his legs over the side and dropped into the water.

The wind had no effect on the state of the water below. He sank rapidly into the underwater world, which he knew so well. With a sigh of relief, he realised that his plotting on the chart had been very accurate. He had dropped right into the middle of the hole and was heading straight for the sunken treasure ship, which was stuck in an upright position between the rocks.

Moments later, his feet touched an iron rail, sticking out from what once had been the ship's deck. He tied the end of the cable tightly to this rail and then climbed over the side of the ship and carefully lowered himself on to the deck. Pieces of broken wood and rusty iron lay scattered about. At the stern of the ship was a large cabin with a hole where once a door had been. Fish swam in and out through this hole, as Ben eased himself towards it, at the same time glancing quickly down at his watch.

He slid through the big hole in the cabin and found himself in the remains of an empty room. At one end, a handrail led down into what he thought must be the hold of the ship.

If there's any treasure, that's where it will be, he thought to himself.

He edged towards the handrail. Down below, it was completely dark. The beam of light from his headlamp shone only halfway down the rusty steps. He grasped a piece of twisted metal and jumped into the blackness beneath him. As his headlamp lit up his landing place, he stiffened in terror.

Beneath him were human skeletons, joined to one another by chains around their necks. His lamp picked out first one, then another and then another, in a line that did not seem to end. Some had collapsed to the left, some to the right, but each skeleton was joined to its neighbour by the heavy iron chain.

His foot touched a large, wooden beam. On one side of him a grinning skull stared with sightless eyes. On the other, a bony hand reached out from a heap of broken bones, as if trying to drag him down into them.

He checked his watch and realised with alarm that he had almost finished the oxygen supply in the first cylinder.

His pounding heart sounded louder and louder and he knew that he must quickly switch over to the extra oxygen supply. He knelt down, pushing aside an outstretched arm. Reaching behind him, he grasped the cylinder valve. He sank back on to his heels, as he felt the life-giving oxygen gush into his mouthpiece. Then he rested.

The sailing-ship had sunk laden with slaves. If there was any treasure, he had very little time left to explore the rest of the ship and look for it. He edged his way towards the far end of the hold, carefully avoiding the piles of human bones around him. As he moved forward, his flipper caught under a length of chain. He bent down to free it and as he did so his headlamp cast a strong beam to his left picking out another staircase. Ben made a great effort to reach it. He was starting to panic now. He knew he should be preparing to return to the surface. He dare not leave it too late. If he did, another slip or fall could prove fatal.

Reaching this new staircase, he pulled himself up towards an opening at the top. With a great effort, he pulled himself through the hole and suddenly his light shone into another room.

As it did so, something glittered in front of him. He took a step forward into the room and looked about him. A heap of bones lay in one corner. They appeared to be the remains of two slaves who were tied together. In the centre of the floor lay the bones of another man. Lying on his crushed skull was a statue of a woman which seemed to be covered with diamonds. It was these diamonds which had glittered in the beam of his lamp, when he entered the room.

Ben tried to think what had happened. Could it have been that, as the ship was sinking, two slaves had managed to free themselves from the long chain of men and killed this man with the statue? Was this a two-hundred-year-old murder?

He bent down and examined the statue. It was a beautiful work of art and could be made of solid gold. Miraculously, it seemed to have been unharmed by its watery burial. He tried to lift it up but the effort was too great and he fell back on to the rotten wooden boards beneath him. One of them gave way under his weight and he suddenly felt the whole floor start to move, as rusty nails parted from rotting wood. One of the timbers floated upwards towards what had been the ceiling of the room.

Struggling to his feet, he looked at his watch. He had only four minutes left. He had to get out of the room quickly and trust that he could find his way back to the place where he had tied the cable.

The wise words of his instructor came back to him: 'In all situations never panic. Remember that, if you panic, you use up oxygen at a faster rate than if you control yourself.'

He eased himself through a broken window and as he did so he heard the oxygen cylinders scrape against the side. There was only just enough room for him to slip through.

Back on deck, he looked for the cable. For a moment he leant on it for support. Then he pulled twice on the cable.

6
The Storm Breaks

The response was immediate. Whatever Mr Moagi's motives for hiring Ben might be, it was clear that he needed him to provide information. As Ben broke the surface and was pulled on to the deck, his only feeling was one of relief. He sat, hunched and still, while the two men removed his breathing apparatus. For a long time he did not speak but sat staring at the eyes of the figure in the hood. Evil though he looked, the relief of establishing human contact overcame his feelings of fear.

'Well, Ben, tell us what you have seen,' the hooded one said eventually, when he was unable to contain himself any longer.

'I never thought I'd be glad to see you again,' Ben managed to say at last. 'Why, you and your

Ben was pulled on to the boat.

friend are as welcome as the first rains after what I've seen down there.'

Back in the cabin, with a glass of beer in his hand, Ben told them all that he had seen. Occasionally the hooded man looked at his companion. When Ben reached the point in the story where he found the statue, he paused. Should he tell them about it? If he said nothing, that might be the end of the matter. If he could convince them that there was no treasure on board, then the whole job might be given up and he could get away from a situation which was becoming far too difficult. But his curiosity got the better of him. Ever since he had trained as a deep-sea diver, he had always dreamt of the day when he would find treasure at the bottom of the sea.

'There was something else,' he said at last.

'Yes?' the man said softly. 'What else did you see?'

Ben hesitated and then told him.

'But why didn't you bring it up with you?'

'Because,' Ben said slowly and deliberately, 'if I had tried to do that I would most likely not be here talking to you now.'

As the questioner released his pent-up breath, the sinister black hood billowed out from his face.

Before either of them could speak further, there was a crash of thunder and a sharp gust of wind rocked the boat. The hooded man turned to his friend, who ran quickly to the controls. He started the boat and it gathered speed.

'High time, too,' said Ben. 'We're crazy still to be out of the safety of the bay. Unless we're careful, we're all going to go down to the bottom of the sea and join those poor slaves.'

'Next time you go down there, you will be well equipped to bring up what we want. We shall make sure you recover the statue.'

'Who said there is going to be a next time?' Ben shouted back over the roaring of the wind and the crashing of the waves against the sides of the motor boat.

'What did you say?' the other said.

'I said, I can't wait to get back down there, now that I know what it's like up here.'

The boat was racing now and the sea was becoming more and more unsettled, causing spray from the waves to crash on to the top of the cabin. Just as they reached the opening to the bay where the camp was situated, the storm broke. For a few minutes, heavy rain beat down on the tiny craft, as they aimed it towards the shore. Mr Moagi was there to meet them as they tied up at the jetty.

The four men hurried into the main hut and, after Anna had brought them beer and food, Ben once again told his story. When he reached the point where he had discovered the statue, Mr Moagi stared at him.

'I knew that you could do it. I tell you, Ben, if you bring that statue up tomorrow, I'll release you from our contract and pay you our agreed sum in full.'

Ben looked up at him. Mr Moagi's eyes had narrowed and he was slowly rubbing his hands together. Ben knew that he had given Mr Moagi information that he had been waiting a long time to hear. He also sensed that he would have to be very careful. Mr Moagi was never more dangerous than when close to success.

'I agree to that,' Ben said. 'The sooner I get away from you and your mad schemes the better. But you must realise one thing: that statue is heavy. I think it's made of solid gold. How that slave managed to pick it up, I do not know. I'll have to take two cables. One for me and one for the statue. It's too great a risk to try to bring us both up on one cable.'

'We'll do as you suggest. He's doing well, isn't he?' Mr Moagi said, turning and staring at his hooded friend. 'I told you that he was the right man for the job.'

The other gave a laugh, which made Ben shiver with fear.

'Yes, and you're right to let him go after he's completed this job.'

He paused and turned towards Ben. 'We shan't need you any more, once you've handed us the statue.'

Mr Moagi started to smile but, when he caught Ben staring at him, he rose to his feet and said, 'You must be tired. Tomorrow you'll leave at dawn. Although I wanted you to dive at night, the weather looks bad and we must finish early. Go and sleep now, Ben. You'll be woken at five.'

Ben went out of the hut and into the warm night. The storm had died away, as quickly as it had blown up, but there were flashes of lightning out to sea and a rumbling of thunder in the distance. He walked towards the tiny hut. There was no light inside and, as he stooped to enter, he heard a loud burst of laughter coming from the hut he had just left. His sense of unease increased.

He could just make out the mat and blanket which had been left at one side of the hut for him to sleep on. He spread these out and lay down to sleep. As his eyes closed, brightly-lit, grinning skulls floated in front of him in a sea of blackness. As they floated past, bony arms stretched out and pulled at him trying to drag him down into the dark sea.

He saw among the skulls one that he recognised. It bobbed up and down, and became more and more swollen until it looked like Mr Moagi's face. It laughed at him and then other skulls reappeared to form a moaning chorus. 'Ben, Ben, Ben,' they called out. Suddenly, a huge, bony arm stretched out and pulled at his arm. 'Ben, Ben, Ben.'

He woke with a start, trembling with fear. 'Go away, go away,' he shouted.

Uncertain whether he was awake or dreaming, he sat upright. Someone was there. He could see a figure in front of him. 'Ben, Ben, Ben,' a voice was saying.

'Who are you? What do you want?'

'Keep your voice down. It's me, Anna.'

7
The Precious Statue

'Anna, what the …?'

'Keep quiet, Ben,' the girl said as she pushed him down and knelt beside him. 'Shut up, please, Ben. They'll kill me if they find me with you. Listen, you're in great danger. You must be careful. I have to tell you that …'

She could say no more. The matting at the front of the hut, which blocked the doorway, was pushed aside and a figure stood there, outlined against the night sky. Anna froze as Mr Moagi called out, 'Hey, Ben, are you all right? I heard some shouting just now. Where are you? I can't see anything.'

'I'm all right,' Ben answered. 'I've had a bad dream, in which you were the star performer. I prefer you in the flesh rather than in my dreams.'

‘Just a minute,’ said Mr Moagi suddenly, ‘I can see more clearly now. Who’s that with you? There’s someone else in there. Who is it? Tell me, who’s in there with you?’

Anna jumped to her feet. ‘It’s only me,’ she said softly. ‘I heard the shouting as well and came to see what the trouble was. I only came to …’

Before she could finish the sentence, Mr Moagi, in spite of his size, had leapt into the hut with the speed of a leopard. Grabbing Anna by the hair, he pulled her towards the entrance. She screamed back at him, ‘No. No. Stop it! Stop it!’

‘You traitor,’ he shouted. ‘You evil girl.’ His fat hand cracked down on the side of her face and she fell to the ground.

‘Go back to your hut, you useless woman,’ he screamed. ‘Go, so that I can beat you.’

She ran, sobbing, in the direction of another hut, with Mr Moagi walking after her. Ben listened, as the thud of his blows and her loud screams drowned the distant thunder. Then all was still, all was quiet. He sank back on to his mat.

She risked a lot to do that, he thought. What was she trying to tell me? She was trying to warn me that my life is in danger. I must get out of here, even if I have to run into the bush. I must get out of here.

He got to his feet and moved towards the doorway. He heard footsteps approaching and then someone coughing. It was the boatman. The footsteps stopped and Ben heard him sit down beside the door. He then started to sing the sad song that Ben had heard on the boat journey to the camp.

So that's that, he thought. They have put a guard on me to make sure that I stay where I am. Poor Anna, if they allow her to live, at least I know I have one friend round here.

The man at the door suddenly stopped singing and Ben heard the rustle of a cigarette packet. A moment later, he heard the sound of a match being struck.

'Have you got a cigarette for me?' he called out. 'I want to go for a short walk.' He heard a click, the unmistakable click of a revolver being cocked.

'Go to sleep and don't make trouble.'

Sleep didn't come easily. For a long time, Ben lay awake, listening to the noise of the man outside. He knew that he wouldn't be able to leave the hut, as long as the man stayed awake. After a while, Ben dozed off into a light but troubled sleep. No sooner had he done so, than he felt his arm being roughly shaken. He opened his eyes and saw Mr Moagi standing over him.

'Come, Ben, it's time to get up.' Mr Moagi was smiling at him. As Ben rose to his feet, Mr Moagi put his large hand on his shoulder. 'Today is your big day. We have some food in the hut ready for you. I have cooked it myself, as Anna is not very well.' The smile vanished, the face hardened and Ben saw him check himself from saying anything more. Very softly he went on, 'Do everything you are told to do and it will be all right. Come.'

Mr Moagi waited while Ben dressed, and didn't stop talking. He pointed out how rich Ben would become after today and how grateful he was that he was helping him in this exciting adventure.

As long as he thinks that Anna did not come to warn me of possible danger, Ben thought, I might not be guarded too closely. I must get away from here.

But there was no chance. What Mr Moagi really thought about Anna's visit to him, Ben never knew. What he did know was that every move he made was closely watched. Never once was he let out of Mr Moagi's sight. Of Anna, there was no sign.

It was getting lighter by the minute as they went down to where the boat was moored. Once again, they left Mr Moagi behind and, as they headed out to sea, Ben watched him waving at them with both hands raised above his head, his shirt tails billowing out behind him in the wind.

The wind worried Ben. It was too fresh for the time of day and he had never in his life heard such thunder rumbling continuously through the night. He felt that a great storm must be building up in the distance. This fact worried him more than all other dangers.

They reached the buoy and once again plotted the distance to the sunken wreck. Ben put on the diving equipment and the boatman helped him with the oxygen cylinders and the headlamp.

They had agreed that the cable, to which he hoped to tie the statue, should be pulled up first and that the signal for this would be two hard tugs. Ben would then grab the other cable and signal that he was ready to come up by giving it three hard pulls. Secretly, he had formed another plan. He felt sure that they intended he should never reach the surface. He was convinced that, once they had got the statue, they would not bother to pull up the second cable. Anna had tried to tell him as much. He knew exactly what he would do. In spite of the risk involved, he planned to tie the statue and himself to the same cable.

As they lowered him into the water, he could see heavy, black, storm clouds gathering on the eastern horizon.

There's a big storm going to break before long, he thought. We'll all be joining those slaves down there, if we're not careful.

He was soon down in a world where there were no storms: the underwater world which he knew so well. The plotting of the position of the wreck was as accurate as before. Within seconds he had landed neatly on the ship's deck. Again he tied the end of the cable to the rail and then, with the second cable grasped firmly in his hand, he moved towards the window of the cabin where the statue lay. Squeezing through the hole, he found himself for a second time among the skeletons in the cabin. He edged towards the treasure and picked it up with two hands. It was very heavy. His job was not easy.

As he picked it up, he noticed with horror that the rotten planking underneath him was giving way. He held out a hand to try and move on to a safer plank but, as he did so, he dropped the diamond covered statue and it slipped down through a big hole. It had sunk into the darkness below and he knew what lay down there!

What could he do now? For a moment he thought about pulling on the cable, so that he could be pulled up and out of the sea. Instead, he decided to go after the statue.

He looked nervously at the pile of bones lying in the corner of the room. The skulls seemed to be staring at him in anger. He felt as though he was stealing something from them and that they were cross about it. His fears returned as he went through the hole. 'Come on, come on,' he said to himself.

Once again he went into the terrifying darkness. His headlamp soon picked out the statue lying on top of a dead slave's ribcage. Summoning all his courage, he swam down towards it. The skulls of the chained skeletons in the hold stared at him as he fastened the cable end around the priceless statue. His blood ran cold as he felt something touch his back. He turned round in time to see a thigh-bone floating off into the darkness. Refusing to allow himself to be frightened, he grasped the statue and floated back up with it towards the deck.

He reached it at last. He wrapped a few metres of cable around his arm and gave two, long pulls. The response was immediate. He felt the cable tighten and both he and the statue were pulled quickly upwards.

This is a heavier load than they expected, he thought grimly.

Suddenly, he noticed the other cable, which was only a metre or two away, go slack and drift downwards. They've cut the cable that I was supposed to be tied to, he thought.

He noticed the water starting to swirl around him. The expected storm had broken. He came to the top of the sea and was immediately banged against the boat, which was being tossed about in the water by strong winds. Waves crashed against its side and he was sucked back into the water.

The hooded man and his friend had tied the wheel of the boat and had both their hands on the winch. The boat was circling helplessly in the waves.

Ben resurfaced and again hit the side of the boat. His arms strained in their sockets, as he struggled to hold on to the cable. The statue, which was fastened to the cable several metres above him, was pulled aboard. With a great effort, Ben managed to grasp the side of the boat and the hooded man immediately let go of the winch and ran up the deck towards him.

At first, Ben thought that he was going to stop and pick up the statue but he ignored it and ran on towards Ben, his hood flapping over his face. When he reached Ben, he raised his boot and brought it crashing down on Ben's hand. Ben withstood the crushing stab of pain but when the man stamped down a second time, he was forced to let go of the cable. He sank below the surface and was immediately caught by a wave and thrown heavily against the boat. At the same moment something crashed heavily into his back, causing him to lose consciousness for a few seconds. Fortunately, the almost empty gas cylinders, which were still tied to his back, kept him afloat.

A large, wooden plank had struck him. In desperation, he tried to cling to it but the boat circled around him at high speed, forcing him to give up the attempt. Once again, he was sucked under water. Convinced that he would soon drown, the men on the boat circled him for a last time and then headed for the shore at high speed.

Ben felt certain that he was going to die. He tried to release the cylinders but he couldn't move; the straps had become hooked on to the wooden plank. Bound tightly to the plank, he was completely helpless. Fortunately, this is what saved him. How many times he was turned over and over by the waves, he never knew. But he always managed to surface long enough to gulp down some air, before being sucked under a wave once again.

As suddenly as the wind had started, it dropped, only to be followed by a downpour of heavy rain. Ben lay exhausted and semi-conscious, as the water became calmer and the rain and hail battered his bruised and bleeding body.

And then the rain stopped, the waves died down to a gentle swell, and the sun came out from behind heavy, black clouds which slowly gave way to patches of bright blue sky. The swell of the sea was carrying him slowly towards the shore. By some miracle, he was being brought ashore alive.

A piece of floating timber banged against the side of his plank. Ben opened his eyes and slowly raised his head. He gasped in amazement at what he saw. The piece of wood was painted white and red and had come off the side of a boat. He was absolutely certain that the boat was the motor boat which had taken them out to sea. Slowly he understood what had happened. They hadn't made it. The boat had been wrecked before they had reached the shore. The statue had returned to the bottom of the sea and, with any luck, the two crew members were there with it. In spite of the danger he was in, he smiled to himself. He had lived and they hadn't.

He could see more pieces of the boat's timber now. They, too, were drifting towards the shore on the gentle flow of the sea. Eventually, he was cast with the other pieces of driftwood on to the shore. For a long time he lay very still, strapped to the plank which had saved his life. He was utterly exhausted.

When he had got back some strength, he unfastened himself from the cylinders and struggled to his feet. His diving suit was torn and his body was cut and bleeding. He was still weak but he slowly managed to free his body from the suit. He felt very relieved that he was alive and he stared for a long time at the cylinders that had saved him.

It was dark when he started to stumble along the beach in the direction of the camp. He felt that he had to try to reach it. If the two men in the boat had been killed, then that left no more than five remaining at the camp, one of whom was Anna. Anna was a friend and he felt certain that he could deal with Mr Moagi. As for the others, for the moment they didn't matter. When they learnt that their mission was in ruins, they would probably run off. They owed their friendship to no one and were simply there for the money.

He stumbled on, wearing only his swimming trunks, his strength slowly returning. In the light of the moon, he saw what appeared to be a pile of clothing lying on the shore ahead of him. As he drew closer, he saw that it was the body of the strange man who had gone with him out to sea with the hooded man. He was dead. Ben shivered, and quickly walked on, but a few moments later he stopped. If I dressed in his clothes, he thought, it might serve as a useful disguise. He walked back to the dead man. Pulling off the wet trousers which the man was wearing, he wrung the water out of them and put them on. He was glad to find several loose coins in the pockets.

Ben had bent down to remove the man's shirt, when he noticed a dark stain on the sand. He paused, and turned the body over. The stain was blood. The man had not drowned. He had been shot in the back, presumably by the hooded man. But when? Before the boat had been wrecked? Had they been fighting over the one lifeboat or over the statue? He forced himself to put on the dead man's blood-stained shirt, with the neat little bullet hole drilled squarely between the shoulders.

Although lightning still lit up the distant sky, the sea was quite calm. He walked along the shore, keeping close to the water. A bright moon came from behind a mass of dark clouds and lit up the scene. Ahead, he could see the sandy shoreline, which was the beginning of the little bay where the camp was situated.

As he came closer, he saw the huts but there was no fire, no noise, no sign of life. As he drew nearer, he grew more cautious, keeping in the shadows of the trees and out of the bright reflection of the moon. All was quiet; nothing moved. He approached the central hut and saw that a fire was smouldering and, on top of it, a pot was steaming. He raised the lid. The contents, whatever they had been, were burnt. Someone had left in a hurry. As he walked round the huts, he could see other signs of a speedy exit. Clothes were left on the ground; nothing had been packed or taken. They had gone; they must have fled. But why the hurry? They would not have left just because the boat had been wrecked, unless someone they didn't want to see had surprised them. They must have got the statue after all.

These thoughts were silenced, for lying in the centre of the floor of the hut was a cloth. As he picked it up, his heart, not for the first time that day, nearly stopped beating. For in his hand he held the black hood. Where was the owner and why was he showing his face to the world? Then Ben suddenly remembered how, when the man had stamped on his fingers, his features had stood out quite clearly as the wind blew the damp cloth against his face. Maybe he was not disfigured after all. Maybe it was just a trick to make sure that Ben didn't know who he was. But why would he bother to hide his identity? It could only be because Ben would know who he was. Either he was famous or someone Ben had met. But if he had met him, he would have tried to conceal his voice and he had never tried to do that. Therefore, he must be a well-known person. He let the hood drop to the ground.

He thought of Anna. Was she alive or had they killed her, too? Mr Moagi would be quite capable of doing that. He walked quickly to the hut where she had slept. It was empty, but quite clearly Anna had left in a hurry too; her things were scattered over the floor. She had quite possibly been taken by force and against her will.

Ben left the hut and walked down to the shore where they had moored the boats. One had been left behind. Fate had been kind to him. But first he must sleep.

8
Journey to Otavi

Twenty-four hours later Ben was back in Walvis Bay. It was dusk when he arrived, and he left the boat in the same spot where the now dead stranger had picked it up.

He walked painfully along the sandy track and into the town. He was tired and hungry. The cuts and bruises which he had received the day before hurt badly. His body ached from rowing the boat. He tried to form a plan. He had little money; he was still sought by the police; he had nowhere to go. As far as he could see, he had two choices: either to forget about the whole affair, go back to his home town and hope never to see Mr Moagi again; or, to track him down and avenge himself for the way he had been treated. Before finally deciding, there was one thing he *could* do. He could go to

Mr Moagi's office and then to his house. As the office was nearer, he would go there first.

The first thing he noticed, when he went up to Mr Moagi's office door, was that the company sign was gone. There was no trace of 'Oil for Namibia'. He looked through the windows at the scene inside. The room was bare; every piece of furniture was gone. Only the ceiling fan remained.

He hurried on to the house where he had met Mr Moagi and signed the contract. Like the office, it was empty. The curtains were gone from the windows; the rooms were clear of furniture. There was no sign of Mr Moagi or, indeed, any evidence that he had ever lived there at all.

'Hey, you, what you doing?'

Ben jumped back from the window, as he felt a hand on his shoulder. He turned round and stared into the face of an evil-looking stranger.

'Are you a thief?' the man went on. 'If so, you're out of luck. This house is empty and has been for a very long time.'

'Look,' Ben said angrily, 'I am not a thief, so get that straight. I'm looking for a man called Mr Moagi. He lived here last week, because I came here and I saw him. At that time there was plenty of furniture here and the house was not empty.'

'You are mad and a liar,' the other replied. 'Get out of here and fast. I own this house and have done so for five years. It's been empty for the last three and I don't know any Mr Moagi. Furthermore, I don't like strangers on my property, so clear off fast or I'll call the police, and tell them that I caught you attempting to break into my house.'

The man meant it, Ben could see that. He said nothing and started to walk away. As he reached the end of the compound, he noticed a piece of paper lying on the drive. He bent down to pick it up. As he did so, the man shouted at him, 'Don't you touch that, get out of here!'

Acting on instinct, Ben grabbed the paper and ran. He heard the other man shouting behind him and dodged quickly to the right and up a narrow road, where there was a collection of small, broken-down houses built of mud and roofed with tin. One of these had partly collapsed and the ground around it was littered with old tins and broken pottery. Nobody seemed to be about, as he crept into the house. He heard the man shouting, 'Stop thief! Stop thief!' and then voices of others taking up the cry. But they quickly faded and slowly the shouting died away.

He closed his eyes and sat quite still, hardly daring to breathe. After a few minutes, he moved closer to the door and unfolded the paper which was screwed up tightly in his hand. It was a receipt from a shop for tins of fruit and meat. Gillani and Shah, he read, 10 Hibiscus Street, Otavi. It was dated the week before, addressed to Mr Moagi and signed Harry Gillani.

Ben had noticed, when he entered Mr Moagi's compound, that it had been very tidy. He knew that when a house is vacated many signs of the owner's rubbish are left behind. Yet someone had gone to a great deal of trouble to get rid of all traces of Mr Moagi's occupation. Why had the man made such a fuss when he saw that Ben had found a piece of paper? Why was Mr Moagi taking such great care to cover his tracks?

At this point, Ben made his decision. He would hunt Mr Moagi down. He would not go back defeated to his village. Somehow he felt that this piece of paper was important. And yet, it was just an ordinary receipt for food from a trading company. But why Otavi, nearly six hundred kilometres to the north? Why would Mr Moagi buy goods from Otavi? There were plenty of places to buy goods in Walvis Bay.

He suddenly remembered something that had happened when he had been to Mr Moagi's office. That telephone call from Arnie in South Africa. He remembered that Mr Moagi had not wanted him to overhear the conversation and had rung back. It was a slight clue but somehow Ben felt that it might mean something. Mr Moagi was mixed up in something, but what? None of it made any sense.

He must get to Otavi. That wouldn't be difficult. He knew that at least five buses left the bus station at Walvis Bay every day for Tsumeb and Grootfontein, stopping at Otavi.

It was now nearly dark and Ben managed to slip quietly out of his hiding place and down towards the trading area and central part of the town. At the bus station, he learnt that a truck was going to Tsumeb with some seats for passengers and was leaving at about five o'clock in the morning. He bought something hot to eat and then settled down in a corner of the bus station to sleep.

There was the usual bustle going on round about him: adults and children selling food and cigarettes; buses and trucks coming in from Keetmanshoop and Windhoek. No one paid any attention to one more person; there were plenty about.

'Bread and biscuits. Bread and biscuits.' A small girl walked past him, stopped, turned round and said quietly, 'Come on, Mister Man, buy some biscuits – only ten cents.'

'OK,' Ben said.

The girl stopped, tore off a piece of newspaper which was tucked under her arm, took the tray off her head and wrapped five biscuits up in the paper for Ben. He gave her the money, she winked at him, and then walked away, her voice calling out her wares as she went.

Ben unwrapped the newspaper and started to eat a biscuit. The girl had given him a part of the front page of a well-known national newspaper. There was a large headline which said, 'Government concern at diamond smuggling – Minister acts.' Ben read the rest of the scrap of paper.

'Minister Pieter Doornskop,' it went on, 'who has just returned from a mission overseas, has expressed the government's grave concern at the activities of smugglers of diamonds and national antiquities. He emphasised in the House that the maximum and severest penalties would be imposed in future. The minister also expressed his concern at the illegal transfer of foreign currency abroad. He said that it had reached such a state that the economy was being severely …' Here the page ended, torn by the biscuit seller, but there did remain part of the photograph of the minister and the newspaper bore yesterday's date.

Well, thought Ben, there's one bit of antiquity smuggling they don't know about! When I catch up with Mr Moagi and get that statue back. I'll make sure that the minister gets it personally in his office. If I hand deliver it, I may get a pardon from the police. He threw the piece of paper away, finished the biscuits and curled up on the ground to sleep.

There were others sleeping round about him. A few of them were travellers waiting for an early morning truck or bus, but most were homeless beggars. Before he dozed off, Ben thought about how low he had sunk. The Namibian Olympic swimming hope, the UK scholarship winner, sleeping rough with beggars in Walvis Bay bus station.

He was awake long before five and, after eating some bread and drinking a cup of tea bought in a corner of the bus station where the cooking seemed to go on all night, he made his way over to the spot where he had been told that he would find the truck for Tsumeb. It was being loaded with large sacks and was surrounded by passengers who were arguing with the parking boys.

Ben joined the crowd, paid his fare and climbed up on to the truck, where wooden benches for passengers were situated in front of the sacks stacked at the back. It was, like most such trucks, being overloaded. Ben sat down in a space on a bench at the back. Determined to attract as little attention to himself as possible, he pulled the tattered shirt, which he had taken from the dead man, tightly round himself, praying that the bloodstains would not be noticed. He looked at the other passengers; they were in high spirits, calling and shouting to each other in different languages.

Suddenly Ben froze. There, seated on a bench in front of him, was the man who had chased him the day before. There was no mistaking him, even in the half light of dawn. Instinctively, Ben felt that he must be on his way to visit Mr Moagi. Ben assessed the situation. He had a piece of paper that could possibly get Mr Moagi into trouble and that man knew it. Quite possibly the man was on his way to warn Mr Moagi.

He could think of no other explanation, unless the man had another reason for going to Tsumeb as quickly as possible. No, the coincidence was too great. He must be going to warn Mr Moagi.

Ben crouched in the shadow of the sacks piled high behind him. He was fairly safe in this half light. But on the journey, in the full light of day, the man would be bound to see him. Somehow, he had to stay on the truck but keep out of sight.

He looked round at the sacks. They were stacked carelessly, with holes and openings in between them. If he could squeeze into one of the holes, he might be able to hide away. In the general bustle and activity, he might not be noticed.

He stood up, waited until the other passengers were not looking, and then climbed up the nearest pile of roped sacks and dropped behind them. As he had thought, the bundles and packages had spaces between them where he could hide. He slid into a space and crouched down.

Minutes later the engine of the truck was started and the vehicle moved forward, every nut and bolt which held it together groaning under the weight of the loads and passengers. The driver's boy, who sat on the tailboard of the truck, climbed up last. It was his job to watch the road behind them, to warn the driver when a vehicle wanted to overtake, and, more important, to keep an eye open for police, who might want to know why the vehicle was carrying a load half as much again as the permitted weight.

The boy suddenly caught sight of Ben. He shouted at him angrily, telling him that he should return to the benches where the other passengers were seated. Ben had not the slightest intention of moving in that direction. Instead, he got to his feet and grabbed hold of the boy's shirt. Then, with a lightning shove of his foot, he pushed hard on the boy's chest. Completely taken by surprise, the boy fell backwards and off the back of the truck.

The truck was gaining speed and passing out through the bus station as the boy landed, with a thud, on his back in the dust below. He sprang to his feet and ran after the truck, shouting and screaming at Ben and to the driver to stop. The shouts were soon drowned by the roar of the truck's diesel engine and the boy disappeared in a blast of fumes from the truck's exhaust.

Ben knew the risk he had taken. The boy might go straight to the police and ask them to set off after the truck and remove the passenger who had kicked him over the side. Ben didn't think that likely; the Walvis Bay police would hardly set out at five a.m., even if they believed the boy's story. He edged his way to the back of the truck and stuck his feet over the side. With any luck, he would be mistaken for the driver's boy.

After about three hours, they came into Omaruru. As they pulled up by the side of the road, they were immediately surrounded by hawkers, young and old, selling all kinds of food and drink. The passengers jumped off to stretch their legs and Ben caught sight of Mr Moagi's friend, as he strolled over to one of the boys selling bread. Ben decided that the best thing for him was to stay exactly where he was and hope that, if any difficult situation developed, he would be able to bluff his way out of it.

For the moment, the driver seemed to be content to stay in his cab. Suddenly, Ben heard the slam of the cab door. The driver slowly walked round the truck and then stared, hands on hips, up at Ben, who was lying flat on his back.

'Have you seen my parking boy?'

'No.'

The man swore and walked away. Ben heaved a huge sigh of relief.

9
The Accident

They were five kilometres from Okaputa, when the crash occurred. One moment they were travelling down a long stretch of road. The next, Ben was aware of splintering wood, screams, shrieks and the useless roaring of the engine, the truck's wheels pawing the air, as if it were an upturned animal. Then silence, more screams and a strong smell of petrol.

Sitting right on the edge of the tailboard of the truck, Ben was thrown completely clear. But the heavy loads and sacks had toppled down on to the passengers, as they were thrown on the ground, and others were pinned under the truck itself. The screams were terrible. Out of the corner of his eye, Ben could see the driver running for all his worth into the bush.

Ben, luckily, had landed on his feet. Two cars had slowed down and the occupants were running towards the accident, wanting to help as best they

Ben was thrown clear of the truck.

could. Ben saw one of them toss a lighted cigarette, as he ran towards the crash.

'Look out!' Ben screamed and then he turned and ran.

The air shook and he flung himself on to the ground, frantically clawing with his hands, in a desperate attempt to cover himself with soft sand. Waves of heat blew over him, as the truck, passengers and loads dissolved in a wall of solid flame.

Ten minutes later, when he felt the heat becoming less strong, he raised himself very carefully and stared back at the remains of the burning truck. A sickly smell of scorched flesh hung in the air; there were no more screams, no more shrieks, just the crackle of the flames and the odd small explosion, as tins and cans blew up in the heat.

Ben realised that the man from Walvis Bay must be dead. He knew, from the position where he had been sitting, that he would have been pinned with the others under the truck. At least Mr Moagi was not going to get the tip-off Ben had feared.

He must get away. The police would be at the scene soon and, as one of the few survivors, the last thing he wanted was to be questioned by the police.

'Move, Ben, move,' he shouted out aloud to himself; but where and how? Another car had pulled up a good distance from the scene of the crash. He raced towards it.

A friendly face looked out of the window. 'Hey,' the man shouted. 'Have you got out of that alive? I don't believe it!' Ben was amazed at how calm the man was. 'They're always crashing at this spot,' he went on. 'Overloaded, worn tyres. They take the corners too fast and whoosh, over she goes. They don't all burn, though. No, they don't all burn.' He shook his head, in mock sorrow. 'I reckon five trucks have crashed at this very spot in the last six months alone.'

'Where are you going to?' Ben asked, ignoring the other man's lack of compassion for the thirty or more bodies which lay burnt and lifeless around the burning wreck. 'Please get me out of here. Give me a lift. I'm trying to get to Otavi.'

For a moment, suspicion flickered round the corners of the man's eyes. 'Yeah,' he said in a mock American drawl, 'you're in a hurry, aren't you. OK, I'll take you there. If you've survived this one, you'll probably manage to get to Otavi in one piece, even with my driving.'

He gave a soft laugh and opened the door at the back of the car. 'I saw some bad crashes in the States,' the man went on. 'Some mighty bad ones but never one that burned. There's always a first time.' He turned round and stared at Ben. 'Call me Joe, son. What's your name?'

'Ben.'

'Where are you going to in Otavi?'

By this time Ben knew two things. He didn't like the man at all and he was going to tell him as little about himself and the happenings of the past three days as possible.

'You can just drop me in the main street,' he answered. 'I'm going to see an old friend of mine.'

'Joe's got the message. Joe will mind his own business.'

Ben stared at the back of the neck of the man in front of him. I might as well stop him asking me questions by asking some myself, he thought. 'Where are you off to?' he said. 'Are you going to Otavi, too, or are you going on somewhere else?'

They were travelling fast now and beads of perspiration were forming on his brow. He noticed that his hands were shaking. Get a grip on yourself, he thought. Take hold, otherwise this guy will get hold of you.

'No, I'm going to Tsumeb,' the other replied. 'Going to meet a guy called Arnie. He's flying in from South Africa or somewhere. Tell you something, son,' he added, 'Joe's honest, he tells the truth. Always trust old Joe, ask him questions, get straight answers. Why don't you try that yourself, Ben. Might do you good, son.'

Ben shut his eyes. No more questions, no more questions please, he prayed. Life isn't like this. How can I have been picked up by a man who is going to Tsumeb to meet a man called Arnie? As he opened his eyes, he saw the other man staring at him through the driving mirror.

'What's up, son, not feeling good? You don't look well, boy. Guess you're suffering from delayed shock. I'll shut up and let you sleep. We'll be there in an hour or so.'

With this, the man pressed his foot even harder on the accelerator and for the next hour he drove like a madman. They shot along the road, screeching round corners, scattering chickens and goats, as they sped through the roadside villages. Narrowly missing a donkey, they had to veer quickly to the left to avoid another car which was racing towards them at an equally dangerous speed.

'I like to see whose nerve gives way first,' said Joe, at one point, as he headed straight at an oncoming car, which pulled on to the side of the road at the last minute. 'Adds excitement to my otherwise quiet existence,' he explained.

By the time they reached the outskirts of Otavi, Ben's nerves were shattered and he shook like a man with fever. Joe slowed down to avoid cyclists and pedestrians, who thronged the streets, or possibly for the police, for there seemed to be many of them.

'Look at all those police guys,' murmured Joe, almost to himself. 'Something's up.' He turned to look at Ben.

'Well, Ben, where's the love nest? Where do you want me to drop you, son? Where exactly are you going?'

'Put me down where you like,' answered Ben. 'But not under the noses of the police, please. I don't want them questioning me about the accident.'

'Or anything else?' Joe added. 'Come off it, you're running away, aren't you? What are you scared of, man? Who is after you? What have you been up to?'

'I don't know what you are talking about,' Ben said. 'Just let me out, please.'

'OK, OK, have it your own way.' He gave a shrug of his shoulders. 'Take this, you never know when you might need your old friend Joe.' He thrust a dirty card into Ben's hand. 'If you're in trouble, come to Uncle Joe.'

Ben got out and Joe drove off.

For a moment he stood still, uncertain where to go or what to do. He was still thinking about the fact that Joe was going to meet a man called Arnie. It was quite likely that there were other men called Arnie who came from South Africa and who did not know Mr Moagi.

His shirt was torn and covered in dust, dirt and oil. He looked a mess but there was nothing that he could do about that at the moment.

The first thing he had to do was to try and find the firm of Gillani and Shah. He guessed it would be in the trading area and the first person he asked told him the way.

It took him about twenty minutes to reach the street which had been pointed out to him. It ran behind a series of low, concrete buildings which stuck out on to the main road. He walked slowly down the street, looking for the name that he wanted.

He soon spotted it. It was similar to the other stores and there seemed to be many customers, both African and European, passing in and out. Outside stood a large Indian. He was standing to one side of the wooden entrance doors and Ben could see him quite clearly from where he was. He guessed that he must be either Gillani or Shah.

He crossed the road and walked slowly up to the entrance doors. The beggars who were sitting outside waiting for small change did not give him a glance. Clearly, in his present state, they did not think that any approach was worth making.

The Indian glanced at him in disgust and Ben felt that he was just about to shout something at him to stop him from going inside, when somebody called out from inside the shop.

'Hey, Harry, come here, we got a complaint.'

The crowd at the door parted and the largest Indian, or indeed, the largest man of any nationality that Ben had ever seen, came from inside.

Bachu Shah had a huge stomach. It bulged over his trousers in not one, but at least three, massive rolls of fat. A belt, which tried to support this huge mass of flesh, flopped loosely in the direction of his thighs.

'Coming, coming,' grunted Harry. 'What's the trouble, what's the trouble?' Wheezing and complaining the other man led him inside.

Ben went into the shop. It was full of shoppers and had the largest number of tins, packets and bottles that he had ever seen. He looked at them, as he walked slowly round. Stacked in pile after pile, they seemed to have been there for years. Some of the labels had fallen apart in the heat, and the tins bulged with gassy fluids. The customers seemed to be paying no attention whatsoever to this mass of old and out-dated tins. All the activity centred on the cold-store at the back of the shop, where he could just see a large freezer full of perishable goods. Harry and Bachu obviously didn't replace the old stock, nor did they worry about getting rid of it.

'Mister Harry, this meat is bad, this meat is rotten, the maggots are making it their home. This place is full of stinking, rotten food.'

Down at the far end of the shop, where the frozen products were kept, a large, middle-aged woman was waving her arms about and shouting. A crowd was gathering around her, to watch the fun, and some were taking her side.

Harry and Bachu Shah walked slowly towards the centre of the crowd. Other shoppers were joining in the shouting and it was clear that a full-scale row was developing. Many of the customers were crowding round the woman and what she had bought.

As Ben walked towards the back of the shop, he noticed an open doorway covered with a curtain. Edging his way towards the opening, he slipped unnoticed behind the curtain. He found himself in a corridor, where a door led out into a courtyard. It was deserted; no one was about; but in one corner stood a small, round, mud hut. Something told Ben to make his way towards it and he chose to do so by carefully working his way round the courtyard wall. There was a small window in one side of the hut, with a wooden frame and shutters. Ben crouched under it and slowly raised his head.

What he saw, took his breath away. There, in a dirty vest and shorts, in front of a huge pile of tins, stood Mr Moagi. His back was turned towards Ben and he appeared to be bending over a small machine which was used for sealing tins.

'A canning factory,' gasped Ben, 'Mr Moagi canning food for Harry. What the … ?

The faint sound behind him made Ben half turn round. But, before he could make out who his assailant was, he was felled with a hard blow to the head. There was a dull, blinding explosion of light which dissolved into a shower of stars. Then everything went black, as he slumped unconscious to the ground.

10
Dog Food!

Very, very slowly the light returned. First he knew about his painful skull; then, as he half opened one eye, a room which turned slowly round and round. Then the room stopped turning and, as he opened the other eye, he saw he was inside Harry and Bachu Shah's shop. He was lying at the end of the shop, where the shouting about the meat had taken place, but now the shop seemed to be empty and it was dark inside. Through the shadows he could just make out a figure standing over him. He saw the grin and recognised Joe.

'Hey, Ben, you wake up now, man. I thought you weren't so innocent and that your little trip to Otavi wasn't quite so unplanned as you made out. Well, well, it hasn't taken long for you to get yourself into big trouble. Yeah, you're a really foolish guy, you sure are.' He turned towards the curtained doorway.

'Hey, Mr Moagi,' he called, 'your friend has woken up; come on over and say hello.'

Ben got to his feet. He heard the sound of feet coming along the corridor. The curtain was pushed aside and the familiar figure of Mr Moagi came from behind it.

'Welcome to Otavi,' Mr Moagi began. 'Is it your first visit here? Really, Ben, I do think that you have gone beyond our contract. It appears that you are trying to travel over land for us as well as under water.'

'Not for you,' Ben said through clenched teeth. His head was throbbing from the blow he had received and he could hardly stand. He leant on the deep-freeze for support.

A gleam came into Mr Moagi's eye. 'You have just given me a wonderful idea, Ben,' he murmured. 'A really wonderful idea.' He stopped short and whispered something to Joe which made him shout with laughter.

'Mr Moagi, your imagination never lets you down. Truly, you are something!'

Ben could see a bulge under Mr Moagi's shirt. He was sure that, hidden there, his hand held a gun and that Mr Moagi was going to shoot him.

'We never thought that you would escape from the wreck, Ben. You are very clever, very strong and I must thank you for finding the statue.'

'Mr Moagi,' said Ben slowly, 'as well as being a thief, you are also a murderer. I found the dead man on the beach and he wasn't drowned. Furthermore, I think you may have killed Anna as well. I'm sure you no longer needed her as her usefulness to you was over. And, by the way, I know that's a gun you've got there. Why don't you bring it out and show it to me before you add a third murder to your list?'

Instead of showing anger, Mr Moagi's face broke out into a happy smile.

'Wrong, Ben, for once you are completely wrong. What I have in mind is far more exciting than a mere shot from a pistol and, furthermore, it's going to give Joe and me some wonderful sport.'

From under his shirt, Mr Moagi took out a strange knife; it had a handle and was about half a metre long. The blades held Ben's attention. There were two of them, both curving in towards the handle but one slightly less curved than the other. They both seemed to be sharpened on each side of the blade.

'What's that?' Ben demanded.

'Well now, Ben, our friend Joe travels a good deal. All over Africa. Out of one country and into another.

Now, as he was crossing through southern Sudan, he discovered this knife in the house of a very old man. You see, Ben, a long, long time ago the old man's forefathers used to live in the hills. At that time, they were raided by men on horseback. His people had no horses, so they made this knife with two blades sharpened on both sides. They would throw this knife at the legs of the attackers' horses. As soon as it hit a leg, whoosh, it sliced it through and the horse dropped to the ground. Now, Ben, Joe has had a lot of practice throwing this knife. He really is quite good, but so far he has had very little experience with a moving target. We thought we would give you the honour of being his living target.'

At this Mr Moagi threw back his head and laughed. His huge, fat body shook with laughter until the tears rolled down his cheeks. Suddenly, he pulled himself together. 'We'll try it in the courtyard,' he said. 'If Joe misses, you can't escape over that wall and he can always pick up the knife and start again. Here, Joe, catch.'

Mr Moagi gave the knife a flick and Ben saw it flying towards him at great speed. He ducked and felt the little gust of air as it whistled past his face. Turning round, he saw Joe catch it in his left hand.

'Oh, well done, Joe, well done,' shouted Mr Moagi, clapping his hands together. 'You see,

Ben, Mr Moagi has learnt a knife trick or two as well.'

There was a sudden crash as a door at the top end of the shop flew open and Bachu Shah, moving at a half run in spite of his size, burst in.

'Get him out and get out yourself,' he cried. 'The police are coming. That woman has complained to the police and they are coming this way. Move fast.'

In a flash Joe caught hold of Ben's arm and bent it up behind his back. He dug his knee sharply into the middle of his back. 'Move, and move fast,' he hissed. 'If you cry out, I'll put this knife through you.'

The pain shot through Ben's shoulder and up into his head. Mr Moagi had already passed through the curtain and into the corridor. As Ben was bundled out after him, he saw Mr Moagi fiddling with the lock of a door at the end of the passage.

'Push him in here,' Mr Moagi called out to Joe, 'and we'll turn the power up. That way we'll get rid of him once and for all.' He flung open a huge, steel-framed door and a wave of frozen air blew into Ben's face.

The freezer, the cold-store freezer, Ben thought in panic. They are going to freeze me to death in the cold-store.

Joe tightened the grip on his arm, placed his foot in the small of Ben's back and, with a mighty shove, sent him into the icy inside of the cold-store. Ben fell on the frosted floor and, before the door slammed shut, he could just hear Mr Moagi's final remark: 'We'll turn you into dog food; at least, that way, we'll make some money out of you.'

11
A Narrow Escape

It was pitch black. No light came through the door and the freezing air cut through Ben's thin clothing, through his skin and into his bones. He knew he could not live for long. At the most, an hour, possibly less; before that he would lose consciousness. He got to his feet and hugged himself tightly; already he could feel the frost forming on his face and hands.

I must move, he thought, I must move. He remembered the police and desperately ran to the big door. He banged on it and shouted.

'Help, help,' he yelled. 'Help me, they're killing me. Help! Help!' He knew it was useless. Even if the whole store was filled with policemen, no one would be able to hear him.

With a great effort, Ben made himself keep moving. For at least five minutes he walked up and down inside his freezing tomb. As he reached one wall, he banged himself against it, to try to keep his body working. Soon he was so cold he could not feel the shock of the banging and the effort became too great. He sank slowly to his knees.

As he did so, he felt his fingers and toes stiffen. Frantically, he tried to move his arms and legs. He fell forward on to his face, at the same time dimly aware of a great burst of light.

'Ben, Ben,' a girl's voice called out. 'Ben, are you alive? Answer me, Ben. Please answer me.'

It was Anna. Unable to answer, unable to speak, he willed himself to raise his head. She rushed towards him. Grabbing him by the feet, she dragged him towards the door. His body was already fixed in the position in which he had fallen and, as she pulled him out and into the passage, he lost consciousness.

Awareness returned. He felt pain in his bones, an unbearable pain which caused him to cry out. Long before he opened his eyes, he felt Anna beside him. Then, as his eyes flickered, she shook him violently.

'Don't worry, it's only the blood starting to circulate again.' She massaged his joints and cried out, 'Don't die, Ben, please don't die; wake up.'

For a long time Ben couldn't speak but his eyes were open now, staring at her pleading face. He slowly became aware that he could talk, when he heard his own voice coming to him, as if from a third person.

'Anna,' he stammered, 'how did you . . .?' But the effort was too great.

'Thank goodness,' she cried out, holding him tightly to her, 'thank goodness they didn't kill you. Listen, Ben, Shah and Gillani were taken off by the police. When Mr Moagi saw them being led away, he disappeared with Joe. I managed to hide in the confusion and, as soon as Mr Moagi left, I got the key to the cold-store and let you out. Another few minutes and you'd have been dead.'

Ben could feel his toes and his fingers now. As the warmth from Anna's body went on strengthening him, he forced himself to sit up.

'Thanks, Anna,' he stammered, his voice a whisper, 'you've saved my life.'

She gently tried to pull him to his feet. 'You must move,' she said. 'It's dangerous here. Someone might come back at any moment. I'm going to lock the freezer door and throw the key away; so, if they come back, they'll think you're still in there.'

She ran off and Ben heard the solid door slam shut. He was getting his strength back and by the time she returned, he could stand without her help.

'Come,' she said, taking his hand, 'follow me.'

She led him into the compound and past the hut where he had seen Mr Moagi and the tins. She pulled him towards another small hut, standing on its own.

Inside, he saw that a gully had been cut through the large, mud compound wall. It acted as a drain and seemed just large enough for a person to squeeze through.

'I managed to make this bigger yesterday without anyone seeing. It's much too dangerous for us to use the front entrance. This way we can get down to the railway line and, with any luck, we'll not be noticed.'

Anna squeezed through the hole and was followed by Ben. Once on the other side, she grabbed his hand and pulled him down a bank, covered with long dry grass. He fell to the ground and lay quite still, letting the warmth of the hot sun seep into his frozen body.

'We can't stay here; someone will discover us. We must make a plan. Now, listen, and I'll tell you what I know. Arnie is coming over from South Africa and is arriving at Tsumeb airport, sometime tonight. Mr Moagi and Joe are trying to get that statue to him, though how they will manage that I don't know. Gillani and Shah are mixed up in it but where they come in, I don't know either. Mr Moagi never told me very much. I just booked the tickets and did what he said. I haven't even seen the statue you brought up but I know they've got it somewhere.'

'But where does the hooded man fit in?'

'I don't know, I just don't know,' Anna replied. 'I'd never seen him, until the day you came. He arrived with the boat, all by himself. Who he is, I haven't a clue.'

'But what about you, Anna. How did you get mixed up with Mr Moagi?'

Before she could reply, a train hooted in the distance. Anna, eyes blazing, turned to Ben.

'That train, it's going to Tsumeb. It's the goods train which always passes here at this time every day. We've got to get on it. It's our only chance of getting there in time.' Before Ben could object, he was pulled to his feet. 'You see where the track bends sharply to the right over there. The train has to slow down on that bend. It has just left the station and won't be going more than twelve kilometres an hour. We've got about two minutes to get down there. Some of the trucks are open wagons and we must jump into one of them without being seen. Come on!'

They ran down the slope and crouched down near the bend in the track. The train was drawing nearer and the rails started to tremble.

'Hide in the grass as the engine passes, so that the driver can't see us,' Anna said. 'Let the engine pass, count eight trucks and then go for the first open one.'

'How do you know all this?' Ben began, but fell silent as the train came into view.

It was travelling quite slowly and, as soon as the engine passed them, they ran out of the long grass and down to the side of the track. The first four trucks were oil tankers, the next four were sealed metal containers. The ninth was open and uncovered.

'Now,' shouted Anna, springing like a hare towards the open truck. She had tucked her skirt up around her waist so that it would not get in the way. With great skill, she was soon on the coupling between the two wagons and was already trying to climb over the side of the truck before Ben had reached the track. The stiffness in his legs made him miss the coupling at his first jump.

'Jump!' Anna screamed. 'Jump!'

He ran forward and sprang up at the coupling between the two trucks but his hands only grazed its side and he crashed down beside the track. Getting to his feet, he saw the look of despair on Anna's face, as the train gathered speed.

He bent low beside the track, watching the wagons coming towards him, sixteen, seventeen and then the guard's van. The guard's van was his only hope. Already he could see the ladder that was fixed to the side for the guard to get up and down.

He bent lower and, as it passed him, he sprang up at it. The open palms of his hands struck an iron rung and he grasped it tightly. For a moment, he was dragged along the ground but, with a final leap, just managed to hook one leg over the bottom rung. The train was gathering speed now. Painfully, he eased himself upright and then climbed up the few steps and looked into the van. The guard was standing, hands on hips, looking back down the track. Ben had already decided that he would need a uniform for the rest of the journey. He slowly moved into the cab and crept up behind the man.

Just as Ben raised his arm to bring his hand down on the back of the man's neck, he half turned round. Unable to stop the blow, Ben's fist crashed on to his windpipe. The man sank to his knees, with an expression of disbelief on his face. Ben grabbed him by the coat.

He was old and fat and certainly in no physical condition to trouble Ben, in spite of his recent experience. Trembling with fear, the man stared at him in terror.

'What do you want?' he wheezed, the blow on his windpipe having taken its toll.

'Just your uniform, then you will leave the train. Come on, get them off.' Ben stood over the unfortunate man, as he removed his trousers.

'I'm sorry, but you've got to leave,' said Ben, staring at the frightened man who was now wearing nothing but a pair of underpants.

'Get off before the train gathers too much speed. Get down that ladder and jump. Hurry or I'll push you.'

The man backed away from Ben, as if he were mad. As he dropped down, falling in the sand below, Ben heard him call out, 'Police! Police!'

He thought about his progress, as he put on the guard's uniform. In twenty-four hours, not only had he kicked a truck boy off the back of a truck, he had also forced a guard off his own train. At this rate he would soon be the most wanted man in Namibia.

12
Tsumeb Airport

When the train reached Tsobis, it stopped just beyond the station. Ben jumped off and ran up to the truck where Anna was hiding. He realized that the guard, whom he had pushed off, must have been able to get a message up the line and the train had been stopped because of that.

He climbed up and over the side of the truck. Anna was not there. Immediately, his self-assurance left him. What was Anna up to? She must have climbed out of the truck, when the train stopped. But why? Was she looking for him or was she leaving him?

Moments later, he heard the sound of brakes and excited voices told him that the police had arrived. There must be at least eight of them, he thought, as he heard them run past his truck towards the engine. It was likely that they had been to the guard's van, found it empty and would soon be checking every wagon on the train.

He had to make a dash for freedom. With Anna gone and the police already after him, it was his only chance. To try and catch Mr Moagi was hopeless. Far better to get out and run into the bush.

Slowly, he climbed up the side of the truck and swung his leg over to lower himself down. As he did so, a strange thing happened. With a jerk, the train started off again and, moreover, began to gain speed in an unusual fashion. Still determined to run for it, Ben lowered himself down towards the coupling.

Just as he did so, he saw the police and they saw him. But nothing happened; there was no shouting, no rifles raised and one of them even gave a friendly wave.

He climbed back into the empty truck, not understanding this. The train now started going much faster. About three kilometres outside Tsumeb, the train slowed down and halted. Minutes later Ben heard Anna's voice.

'Ben, Ben, come out if you are still in there!' Her head appeared over the side of the truck.

'Anna, what is going on?' Ben looked at her as she gave him a half smile.

'Explanations later, action now. Come on, Ben, we must move. We have exactly thirty minutes to get to Tsumeb airport before the plane carrying Arnie arrives. If you want to stop that statue of yours leaving the country, get out of this truck and follow me.'

Ben leapt over the side of the truck. Anna was already running up the bank by the railway. As he climbed up it to join her, she stopped, turned, and waved at the driver. Immediately the engine started moving forward. 'How do you make friends so suddenly?' Ben asked, mystified.

'I'll explain later; come on.' Anna grabbed him by the hand and they ran towards a few houses on the outskirts of the town. She ran up to a car which seemed to be waiting by the side of the road.

'Tsumeb airport,' she commanded and without a murmur the driver opened the door and let them in. More mystified than ever, Ben held his breath as they raced towards the airport. This car was not a taxi and Anna was being treated with a great deal of respect.

At one point, they were held up by a traffic jam. Immediately, the driver reversed and took another route through dusty, bumpy back streets.

'Just in time,' muttered Anna as they came to a halt outside the main airport building. At a run, she led him through a side door, up a corridor and into a small room. A man at the desk, a customs official, gave her a huge grin of welcome.

'Hello, Anna, welcome. So this is your friend. We can talk later. Here's the key.' He tossed her a small key which he had taken out of his pocket.

'Thanks, Peter,' she said, catching it easily. 'Come on, Ben, no time to lose.'

Back in the corridor, she led him up another flight of steps which ended outside a door marked 'Private'. She unlocked the door with the key and pulled him into the small room.

'This is the observation room,' she said. 'Just right for our purposes. Look.'

She pulled aside a small sliding panel and Ben found himself staring down at the customs area.

'Bullet-proof glass; you can see out, they can't see you; very useful to catch smugglers before they smuggle.'

'But how ...?' began Ben.

She smiled at him and held her finger up to his lips. 'Shh, not now,' she said. 'Just look and watch.'

Ben scanned the area. It showed quite clearly the customs hall and the spectators just outside waiting to meet the passengers off the plane.

'Look,' said Ben, 'there's Mr Moagi and I think that's Joe with him.'

Ben could see Mr Moagi leaning against two crates, talking earnestly to Joe.

'Take a closer look,' said Anna, handing him a pair of binoculars.

Ben took the binoculars and stared down at the two men. They seem to be arguing and Mr Moagi had started to wave his hands around wildly.

'Just a minute,' whispered Ben, 'those small crates they are leaning against, they are stamped Gillani and Shah Food Exporters, Namibia.'

'Let me see,' said Anna, grabbing the binoculars out of his hands. 'Yes,' she said slowly, 'yes, now I begin to understand. I think I can see why Harry Gillani and Bachu Shah operate a small canning factory at the back of their shop. It's all beginning to make sense. Hey, wait a minute. Look, Ben, the passengers are starting to come in. I think our plane's landed. I must make a quick telephone call.'

She reached for a telephone which stood on a shelf by the window. 'Peter, get your boys round the back of the arrival lounge and keep an eye on those two small crates. When I tell you, I want the fat man and his friend, who are leaning on them, held and searched. I want those crates opened and I want a gentleman called Arnie held as well.'

Ben listened to her in amazement.

'Don't tell the boys until I give the word. OK?' She put down the receiver and, before Ben could open his mouth, went on: 'In a few minutes the passengers will start coming through. When you see that happen, watch out for Arnie. He will make a move towards Joe and Mr Moagi.'

The baggage had come now and was being carried to the wooden table in front of the customs men. Gradually the passengers passed through to claim their luggage and undergo inspection. Suddenly, at the end of the hall furthest from the entrance from immigration, shouting and scuffling broke out and a man was seen running away with a suitcase.

'What the ...?' began Ben.

'One of the boys has tried to steal someone's baggage. Look, look,' said Anna, 'everybody is joining in.'

The man had been caught, and customs officials and passengers were standing round in a circle. The man was being led away by an airport official.

'The fool,' said Anna, 'he must have known he would be caught with all these officials around. I can't understand people who ...' She stopped suddenly and grabbed Ben by the sleeve. 'They've gone, Ben, they've gone. That was a deliberate diversion. Look, Mr Moagi, Joe and their loads have disappeared.'

It was true. There was no longer any sign of Mr Moagi and the small crates had vanished.

She dashed out of the room, closely followed by Ben. In a moment they were in the customs area among the passengers.

'Hey, where are you going?' shouted an irate official, as they moved towards the immigration area.

'Silence, you fool,' shouted Anna. 'Don't you know who I am?' For a moment she stopped, turned back the lapel of her blouse and showed him a small badge which was pinned on the inside.

'Sorry, sorry,' the official stammered, apologetically.

'I'll make you sorry, you idiot,' shouted Anna, dragging Ben into the immigration room. The waiting passengers parted, as they ran out on to the airport tarmac.

For a moment Anna paused, staring at the jet which had by now been loaded and was preparing to take off. A luggage van was returning empty, having loaded the passengers' goods on to the plane. Anna stood in front of the van and then ran up to the driver.

'Stop, stop,' she shouted. The man slowed down. 'What have you put on that plane? Were there two crates among the people's luggage?'

'Yes,' said the man.

'And where is that plane going to?'

'It's returning to Johannesburg.'

Anna turned and stared at Ben. 'Fool that I am. You see, Arnie never got off. He's doing round trips, collecting the goods on the way. They've put the crates on board.'

With a roar, the jet started to taxi out towards the runway.

'Look,' Anna went on, 'there's Mr Moagi and Joe among that crowd of airport workers. Oh goodness, what can I do? I must stop the plane and catch Arnie. I must get to the control tower and stop that plane. If you tried, you would be arrested. Follow Mr Moagi and Joe. Don't let them out of your sight. My boys are at all the exits and they can't get away. Don't let them see you, whatever you do. Your railway uniform should help.'

In a moment she was gone, sprinting like an Olympic runner towards the control tower. Already the plane had reached the position on the runway for take-off and was waiting for final clearance to depart.

Ben moved carefully towards Mr Moagi, keeping out of his sight but never losing sight of him. He stood staring out at the aircraft, as the roar of the engines got louder.

'Please make it, Anna,' Ben prayed, but a swift glance over his shoulder told him that she had not been able to get there in time. With a roar, the plane taxied down the runway and lifted off into the air.

Not daring to take his eyes off Mr Moagi, Ben watched him, as he waved one fat arm in a farewell salute, placed the other on Joe's shoulder and walked with him towards the passenger lounge. Before they disappeared inside, they stopped and looked round. Ben dodged behind a pillar and watched as they turned towards a flight of steps which led to a bar.

Ben followed them up the steps and watched in the doorway as they sat down at a table and ordered beer. They seemed very happy and joked and slapped each other's backs. Clearly they were delighted at the success of their mission.

And so they should be, observed Ben gloomily. With that statue in one of those crates, it could be worth a lot of money.

'Hey! Don't you stand there, either sit down or go downstairs. I've been watching you, what are you up to? You lost your train or something?' A tough-looking policeman stood behind Ben and, before Ben could say anything, he went on: 'What you doing here? Are you looking for someone or what?' The eyes of all the people in the bar had turned on Ben.

Out of the corner of his eye, Ben could see Mr Moagi looking at him with surprise.

Before he could answer further, Mr Moagi was on his feet, shouting, 'Why, Ben, Ben, how good to see you. I thought you had gone to a colder climate, but it appears you have joined the railways. Now officer,' he said, turning to the policeman, who was now looking confused, 'this is an old friend of mine; he has been looking for me. He is quite harmless and a true, honest Namibian, I assure you.'

As the policeman shrugged his shoulders and turned away, Mr Moagi caught hold of Ben's arm in a strong grip and led him towards the table, where Joe was sitting.

Joe stared at him with cold eyes. 'Thought you'd left us, man,' he said. 'Guess you have a great skill at survival. How do you do it? I ain't known you long but you've used up three lives in two days.'

'Well now,' Mr Moagi began, 'come along, Ben, tell me how you happen to be here.' There was no mistaking the menace in his voice. His eyes had narrowed to slits and his fingernails bit deeply into Ben's flesh.

Before he could reply, there was a roar as a plane touched down on the tarmac and thrust its engines into reverse.

'What the ...?' said Joe. 'What's that plane doing here? There's not another one due for three hours.'

Ben paused and then turned and stared straight at Mr Moagi. 'They've brought Arnie back, Mr Moagi. His plane has returned to Tsumeb.'

Mr Moagi stood up, knocking an empty bottle to the ground. In a flash, Joe had bent down, picked up the broken neck and was holding it closely in front of Ben's face.

'This is your work, son,' he hissed. 'I'm going to carve you up, so that your own mother won't know you.'

'Stop!'

Anna's voice made them all turn round. She held a pistol which was pointed straight at Joe. He dropped the bottle. Behind Anna were at least twenty airport officials and police, many of them armed, and they quickly surrounded the three of them.

'OK, boys, take those two and hold them downstairs. I've got a list of charges against them as long as my arm. Two of you go to the plane and wait for the crates to be unloaded. But don't open them until we are all there.'

She gently put her hand on top of Ben's. 'Well done, I thought you were going to be cut up into pieces. Well, that accounts for two of them, but we've still one or two more to find. You see, Ben, I am in the anti-smuggling squad. The organisation exists to catch high-level, international crooks who smuggle out diamonds and illegal goods and fiddle our exchange control regulations. I got myself a job with Mr Moagi at Walvis Bay, because we thought that he was smuggling diamonds. The only way I could find out what he was up to was by working for him. It took some doing. I couldn't tell you earlier, until I knew whether I could trust you. Well, I know a lot about you now and one thing I can tell you is that the charge the police wanted you for has been dropped. Mr Moagi deliberately had you framed for robbery, so that he could get you into his clutches. There were enough letters on file to prove that to the Commissioner of Police himself!'

Ben could hear Mr Moagi arguing loudly as he was led away. He turned to face Anna.

'I certainly owe you an apology. I just took you for a good-time girl in Mr Moagi's employ. I couldn't think what you saw in the fat toad.'

Anna grinned. 'I had to be a good actress. Come, don't let's waste time talking. The crates should be coming off the plane now, together with Arnie.'

He followed her back down to the baggage area. When they got there, they saw that the two crates had already arrived. Mr Moagi and Joe were standing with a group of about twenty different airport officials and police officers, two of them armed. One of the armed men was holding a small, dark-haired white man tightly by the arm. His small eyes were moving back and forth from Mr Moagi to Joe. But Mr Moagi, who had fallen into a sullen, silent mood, paid no attention to him.

'Come on,' said Ben, 'let's open the crates. Who's got a wrench?'

The first crate was split open and a tin rolled out on to the floor, followed by another, and then another.

'I told you,' muttered Mr Moagi, 'I told you, just tinned fruit, that's all.' His spirits rose visibly, as he tried to convince them of his innocence. 'Look, fruit, good Namibian fruit. Is it a criminal offence to earn good, foreign currency for my country?'

Anna ordered the tins to be opened.

Most of the tins bore labels of Namibian products. There was one larger tin labelled 'powdered milk' which stood in the middle of the crate.

The first tin was opened and Mr Moagi looked on in triumph as chunks of pineapple spilt on to the floor. Then a second tin and a third, all containing fruit of various descriptions.

Then Anna had them open a tin with no label. As the customs officer opened it, he shook it violently and five diamonds dropped on to the floor.

'Try the big one; I think I know what's in it,' said Anna.

As the lid came away, Ben bent forward and saw again what he had seen a few days before in the horrific scene under the sea – the statue.

'That's it, we've got it,' said Anna with joy. 'Take them all away to the police station. We'll open all these tins and let you know just how big the charge list will be. My guess is it will be long enough for a fifteen-year prison sentence for each of them, plus, of course, attempted murder of my friend here and the murder of others unknown.'

As Mr Moagi, Joe and Arnie were led away, and Anna and the remaining officers resumed their tin opening, Ben tapped Anna on the arm.

'There's one person missing, Anna, the one I'd like to get hold of – our hooded friend.'

'That's it, we've got it,' said Anna.

13
An Unexpected Turn

After the tensions of the past few days, even the noise of Windhoek and its traffic seemed relaxing to Ben. As he looked out on to the busy streets from the window of the police saloon car, he heaved a deep sigh of relief, not so much that his recent ordeal was over, but that he was free. Noticing his mood and sharing it herself, Anna threw back her head and laughed.

'Well, who would have thought that only a few days ago I saved you from freezing to death, and here we are going to the minister himself to receive his personal thanks.'

The car drove in through the open gates of the ministry. It stopped outside the front of the imposing office building and two uniformed policemen sprang to attention and opened the door.

'They could both have been guarding my cell door, if it had not been for you!' Ben remarked.

The escort took them up two flights of stairs and then halted outside a large door marked 'Minister'.

'Come in, come in,' said a private secretary who came to meet them. 'Come in, the minister is expecting you.'

They were led into a large room, empty of furniture except for two chairs and a long desk at the far end behind which sat a solitary figure. The curtains were drawn and it was dark, cool and still, unlike the street outside. Only the noise of the air-conditioner broke the silence.

The man rose and stretched out his hand in greeting. Ben noticed the statue, standing at one end of his desk.

'Welcome to the heroes of the hour,' the man boomed. Then he turned to Anna. 'You've worked wonders and fully justified all our confidence in you. The work you have done for our country is of great value; and as for this,' he said, pointing to the statue, 'it is beyond price. I even find the story of its discovery quite hard to believe.'

'Yes,' said Anna, 'that's all thanks to Ben here. He was the one who had the most dangerous and difficult task of all. I just tied the parcel up at the end.'

The two of them laughed loudly and turned to look at Ben. Ben was staring hard at the statue as if he had not heard a thing they had said.

‘Come, Ben,’ whispered Anna, ‘speak to him, remember where you are.’

Ben looked up at the man who was smiling at him. He stared hard into his eyes and suddenly something seemed to jerk inside him.

‘That’s not it,’ Ben said slowly, ‘it’s not the statue I found. I handled it more than anyone and, although that’s a good imitation, that’s not the statue.’ He bent over to pick it up.

‘Stop!’ said the minister. ‘Are you crazy? Have you gone out of your mind, Ben? Of course it’s the statue. The very one that the police brought to me.’

But Ben wouldn’t stop. In spite of Anna’s shout of protest, he had already bent over the minister’s desk and picked up the statue.

‘It’s hollow, it’s a copy, it’s not the one,’ the words tumbled out, as the other two stared at him in alarm.

‘You must be crazy, Ben,’ said Anna. ‘You don’t know what you’re saying.’

Ben saw the flash of steel and with all his force hurled the statue at the minister’s head. It struck home, but not before the whirling knife had cut deep into his shoulder. He felt the steel rip into his flesh like a cold icicle and, in agony, he sank to the floor. As he lost consciousness, he heard the shot.

14
Caught!

Anna was the first visitor the hospital allowed him to see. 'Hello,' she said, with a grin, 'how are you feeling?'

Ben smiled at her. 'They say they'll save my arm,' he said, 'although it won't be quite the same. What happened anyway? After the throwing knife hit me, I don't remember a thing. All I can remember is looking into the eyes of the minister and knowing that he was the same man who had been wearing the hood. I had to throw the statue at him.'

'Well, it was a good throw,' Anna replied with a laugh. 'It hit him full in the face and just gave me time to shoot him in the leg. Luckily, no one heard my pistol shot, because of the noisy air-conditioning, otherwise his bodyguard would have shot us both.

One doesn't usually shoot a minister and get away with it. After I'd wounded him, I had no time to attend to you. I had to see if I could find his hood, because it was the only evidence that would save us. I prayed that there *would* be a second hood somewhere after you'd told me that you'd picked one up in the camp. I took his keys, opened his office safe and there it was together with letters to Mr Moagi which confirmed that he was the leader of the whole racket. From his position of privilege and power, he was able to supervise the whole operation. Who, after all, would suspect a minister? By the way, the police have picked up Harry and Shah trying to cross into Botswana. It was quick thinking on your part to pretend it was an imitation statue; you threw him right off his guard. That statue deserves a special place of honour all to itself in our national museum,' said Anna with a smile.

'And so do I,' murmured Ben.

Fun things to do

Finding out more about **words** can be a lot of fun! **A dictionary** is useful for this.

★ **KEY words** – these are **important** words because they work like a key and can unlock information. They sum up **main ideas**.

What keyword could be used to describe the theme of 'Dead Men's Bones'? (A clue – look at the blurb on the back cover …)

★ ★ ★ ★

It's **smuggling** – to import or export goods without paying customs duties. (That's what Mr Moagi was doing.)

★ On the next page, find the best match in **Box B** for each **keyword** in **Box A**.

Box A	Box B
• diving	• sending goods out of a country
• escaping	• acting dishonestly
• exporting	• plunging headfirst into water
• cheating	• bringing goods into a country
• importing	• getting free

★ Languages are ALIVE and they keep on growing and changing just like YOU do.

They belong to different FAMILIES just like you do, too!

★ **ROOT words** – new words grow out of these.

Smuggle grew out of earlier words *smuckle*, and Low German words *smukkeln* and *smuggelen*. ★ Use these words as ROOTS and find others that have grown from them.

key, land, home, ship, man, finger … then try some of your own.

★ **RELATED words** can be found all over the world! There are at least 6,000 recognised languages in the world.

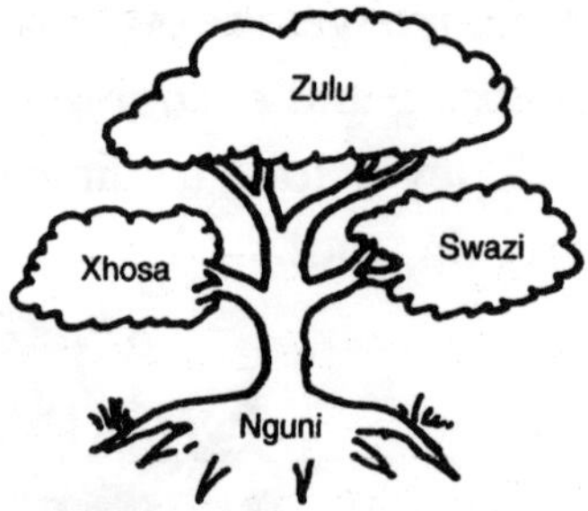

Some of the smaller ones are dying out – a pity! English often replaces other languages as it is such a strong, popular language. It belongs to the Indo-European language family.

Here are a few related words. Find others …
mama, moeder, mother, mutter …
house, huis, haus …
milk, melk, milch …

Find out more about smuggling:

- it's been happening for over 1,000 years.
- all sorts of things can be smuggled – jewels, drugs, cars, lace, wool, people, drinks, animals, ivory, tobacco … etc.
- it can be dangerous and some people seem to enjoy the excitement it brings.
- early smugglers were called 'owlers' because they always worked at night and their signal for each other was the hooting of an owl.

Ways of smuggling:

In 'Dead Men's Bones' the precious statue was hidden inside a large tin of milk powder.

Smugglers nowadays have many other ways of hiding things.

Here are some of them:

inside a cigar

inside a tube of toothpaste

inside chocolates

pages cut away inside a book

inside
the lining of
a suitcase

inside
plastic bags

inside
the sole of a
shoe

secret compartments
under a car